Climate Worrier

About the author

Colm O'Regan is the author of six best-selling fiction and non-fiction books including the *Ann Devine* novels, *Bolloxology* and *The Book of Irish Mammies*. As a stand-up comedian, he has performed all over the world. He has written comedy for TV and Radio and has a weekly column for the *Irish Examiner*. He has a maths podcast called The Function Room which he started during the pandemic because that's the kind of thing that happens. He is currently studying for an M.Lit (Masters in Picking Up Litter) in Inchicore in Dublin where he lives with his family.

Climate Worrier

A Hypocrite's Guide to Saving the Planet

Colm O'Regan

HarperCollins*Ireland*

HarperCollins*Ireland*
2nd Floor Macken House
39-40 Mayor Street Upper
Dublin DO1 C9W8
Ireland

A division of
HarperCollins*Publishers* Ltd
1 London Bridge Street
London SE1 9GF

The edition published by HarperCollins*Ireland* 2023

1

First published by HarperCollins*Ireland* 2022

A catalogue record for this book is available from the British Library

ISBN: 978-0-00-853490-5 (PB)

Typeset by Palimpsest Book Production Ltd, Falkirk, Stirlingshire

Printed and bound in the UK using 100% Renewable Electricity
at CPI Group (UK) Ltd, Croydon CRO 4YY

MIX
Paper | Supporting
responsible forestry
FSC™ C007454

To Dada, a gentleman and a gentle man

Contents

0.

Foreword is Forearmed

'70 bales of cocaine? It'll be the most bales saved anywhere this summer'

– Dada's joke about when bales of cocaine were plucked from the sea one wet summer a few years ago.

I told that joke one night while the cocaine bales were still fresh and the summer was still wet and the audience laughed more at it than the ones I wrote myself. Dada was in the audience and he was fierce chuffed. Every so often Dada could turn out a well-crafted line with the best of them (if you pretend I'm the best of them). He's a big part of the reason I'm writing this book. A 'tasty' farmer with a love of nature and trees but also a tidy farm, he was someone who, like me – and, I assume, like lots of people – had some contradictory positions on the environment. But he was also a man who loved to learn and didn't take it personally when presented with new opinions on the way of doing things. I want to be more like him as I grow up. A bit more useful.

So, what's all this about? This book is my attempt to get a handle on how I, a hypocrite, can help. Me, with my inconsistent views, carbon coming out of every orifice, a western consumer with expectations of how life should go that exceed what the planet is able for, and a fella who's not naturally good with conflict and campaigning and generally growing a pair: how do I do my bit? As a born worrier who has been wallowing in the bad news about nature and the climate over the past decade, I can't unknow the depressing stuff I've read and heard. And of course, I'm a hypocrite, compromised by living in our society, on this planet, earning a living. But I'm stuck with it now. At the end of the day, doing nothing is harder.

The book has ten chapters.

- Chapter 1 isn't very climatey. There wouldn't be much carbon sequestration going on. It's just to give you an idea of where I'm coming from, how that shapes how I think, and why it's hard to think differently.

- In chapter 2 I wade into the stew of talking about food. There are beefs and hot potatoes.

- Chapter 3 is all about the various means and ways of getting around the place and what we might do to save the bitta petrol.

- Chapter 4 is SO ME. An ode to the joy of Getting The Value Out Of A Thing. Buying less stuff, getting things fixed and so on.

- Chapter 5 is about nature and my tentative steps to . . . make some.

- In Chapter 6 I finally get off my arse doing a bit around the place and I discover a way that helps me think about doing a bit more.

- Chapter 7 is about the children, where I have the blinding insight that maybe it's unfair they have to deal with a problem they didn't create.

- In Chapter 8, how I've tried not to lose my sanity in The Debate.

- Chapter 9 talks about energy and inequality. But don't worry, the Banter doesn't stop!

- Chapter 10 is about care without despair, keeping going when it looks pointless. In fact, learning to live with pointlessness has helped me a lot.

- And finally, the Little Book of Colm: a quick summary of my personal philosophy (I know, I know) which may be of no use to you in your situation but if you can't wax philosophical in your own book then WHAT ARE WE? ANIMALS?

It's important to say: I don't know much about anything. I have a bit of lived experience, some minor expertise in comedy, writing, getting cattle out of marshes and tut-tutting over litter, but most importantly, I'm nosy. If you read one book about fixing climate change, don't make it this one. There are specialists in all sorts of areas waiting to take your call. I won't be telling you how to make your own newt-friendly bleach or how to make it as hard as possible for the forces of Disaster Capitalism to throw you out of the foyer of a fossil-fuel-underwriting insurance company. If you're looking for that, I may be a disappointment to you.

BUT there has to be room for the hypocrites to do a bit, to grow into the role of being part of the solution. Even if at the start it's just making tea for the rescuers.

* * *

I don't want to sell hopium. Things are bad. But if humans have managed to create this mess, then maybe we can undo some of it. Me composting won't amount to a rotting hill of beans. But maybe if we're all talking and sharing ideas about where we can start, we can play our individual parts. Stressing about your individual carbon footprint is not the whole solution. In fact, some would argue that it's a ruse to distract, making you focus on your personal sins while Big Everything tries to get away with doing nothing. 'Doing my bit' is mainly about learning. And learning means sometimes getting it wrong the first time.

I want you to smirk, giggle, laugh, nod knowingly and hopefully see something that sparks a thought. Oh, and a quick note about Some Bad Language. Swearing is of course neither big nor clever but sometimes it is necessary. And if you can't swear about the imminent collapse of nature and the potential unliveability of the planet, then what the fuck can you swear about?

1.

You have to see where
I'm coming from

'These bloody cattle would break your heart'

– Dada

The doorbell. Who'd be calling during *Coronation Street*? There's no good reason. We're not Visitor People. Our stated position is: *The house is just not set up for it.* So, when someone calls – and particularly during *Coronation Street* – shit must be going down.

It's the back door, obviously. The back door is how you get into a lot of houses in rural Ireland. The front door was for presidents and popes and awkward furniture. Like a lot of farmhouses, our back door led to a back kitchen – a classic of the genre of damp, badly designed flat-roof extensions of the mid-twentieth century. Built with mass concrete and no insulation of any description, in damp weather the interiors were like those water walls you see in hotel lobbies. But at least it gave us a bit of a buffer before the visitor could see the rest of the house.

I peek out the curtained window to be sure it isn't the squad car. In fifty years, a squad car came into the yard only once, and that was to decommission my father's 'for crows and pigeons' shotgun, an event that was not supervised by a former Scandinavian prime minister. Ours has been a drama-free existence. This time it's a neighbour. He's not selling raffle tickets or collecting petrol money for the priest. He has news.

'Yere cattle have broken into Mary's Bog,' says the neighbour. Well, sugar and shite anyway. Someone orders one of Betty's hotpots on *Coronation Street*. Jack Duckworth wrinkles his nose in exasperation. But what happened next would have to be described to us by Mama when we got back.

It wasn't our first rodeo. The Achilles' hoof of the farmer, cattle breaking out. Cows don't break out now as much as they used to. On a lot of farms, gates are better, there is more wire and fencing everywhere, cows are marshalled between paddocks, rostered. Electric fences line the ditches because it's easier to drive fenceposts than it used to be, and electric fences are better quality and cheaper – and don't cause the interference on long-wave radio. And farms are bigger, so cows are further from boundaries. There are still a few small farms, though, like our one, on which the cows mooch around, pucking each other, accidentally uncovering weaknesses in ditches, acting all innocent. *Oops, did we accidentally get through that gap in the ditch? How silly of us! No, we've no idea how to get back in. The best thing for us to do now is to run as fast as possible in the opposite direction.* There's a point when you're chasing cattle when it really looks like they're taking the piss and laughing at you. For a few hours, they de-domesticate. The last dance of a wedding, auroch the boat.

Cattle broke out in various ways – across other farmland, along a road – but the worst was if they got into a non-farming neighbour's lawn. There is nothing like the mortification of retrieving cows after they've shat all over a nice sward, their besplattered arses jarring the trellises. If you're lucky there would be a slightly stilted conversation with the owners: *Sorry about that/Ah, that's grand.* Hopefully not someone roaring, GET THEM COWS OUT OF HERE BEFORE I CALL THE SERGEANT. But most likely they'd be nice people with more than two trousers and a colour telly and us standing there looking like Tom Sawyer in wellingtons. They know it's part and parcel of living in the farming frontiers of the countryside. But, still, cows shouldn't be coming over the border grazing herbaceously.

This time there was no immediate danger of scutter in the nasturtiums. But they had broken into the river. This was bad from a strategic point of view: they now had access to a major arterial route.

Our farm is on one side of the valley of the River Dripsey. You come out the door, through the haggard, and can run full pelt down a steep, shaley, furzey hill to the Mill Road, and across it down into the Inch. And it was the Inch out of which they'd gone. An inch is a river field. The river Dripsey sweats blackly up out of boggy ground in the Boggeragh Mountains. There's a Sitka spruce forest there now, but it used to be where you'd cut turf (Ireland's slash and burn). The Dripsey winds its way down from the hills of mid-Cork before getting to Carraignamuck Castle, or the rock of the pigs – so-called because, hundreds of years ago, it was a place where pigs were slaughtered. On a rock. Now that set-up would be called artisan, and there'd be a photo of the farmer high above the aisles in Aldi. Although, he would not look Tarantino-ed, and the river in the background would not run red with offal.

That's where you'll find Dripsey Castle, a boutique wedding venue now, originally built by Cormac Laidir McCarthy as a 'companion piece' to the more famous Blarney Castle. Blarney may have the stone to give you the gift of the gab, but in Dripsey we don't be telling anyone our business. Five hundred years ago it was the centre of a legal dispute between Irish chieftains. Cormac's brother Kallaghan said he should have got the castle in Cormac's will and he sued Cormac's sons. Brehon law didn't handle that kind of thing, so the case was held in Dublin under English law – an early form of libel tourism. The will is in Trinity, so if you can prove you're a descendant, there's no better country to put in a claim. Our solicitors are standing by the phones waiting to take your call.

But, mainly, Dripsey Castle is famous because Gabriel Byrne made a film there once for Channel 4. It was called *Reflections* and is about a man who is writing a biography of Isaac Newton and stays in a castle. Long before Channel 4's phase of programmes with titles like *I Hate Your Face* and *Embarrassing Willies*, it was chiefly known for highbrow slow-moving programmes with a plentiful supply of riding. The latter came as a surprise to some Dripsey families who allowed their children to stay up late to watch *Reflections* and saw the smouldering sexpot from the early eighties rural soap opera *Bracken* in a ménage-a-trois-and-a-bit with members of a wealthy Anglo-Irish family in decline, confirming all our hopes and dreams about what goes on in Big Houses and how Church of Ireland people have less hang-ups about That Sort of Thing. I was packed off to bed as soon as the first breast appeared.

Meanwhile, back to Victorian energy generation: the river was harnessed into a millrace to provide power for Dripsey Woollen Mills, which was once famous for its blankets – the cream ones with the pink trim that your granny may have at the top of the hot press and are brought out when people are staying for the removal. Speaking of removal, the woollen mills closed in the eighties when it was fashionable to close every industry in Cork and replace it with emigration and a thriving post-punk music scene. And also it somehow was cheaper to bring in wool from New Zealand. Because we like to bring things in from far away that we make ourselves down the road.

Downstream of the mill is a bit of boggy wood called Mary's Bog – named after a local woman. And below Mary's Bog is our Inch: a beautiful river meadow that has never been ploughed that I can remember. But having land next to a river is like having an independent TD in your government. It makes things more interesting but, in the end, structurally much weaker. In summer the river was low enough to enable bullocks to go on a bit of walkabout. Bulls and cows will wander looking for love; bullocks – having been rendered useless as love machines – just head off for the adventure. A sort of stag. And just like a stag, with displays of bovo-eroticism along the way. Up the river they went and made land at Mary's Bog. If property developers had spotted Mary's Bog during the boom it would have become an apartment complex called Riverbank Villas – the final word in gracious living. And it would have flooded every year and there would have been an inquiry that found no one responsible. Thankfully they didn't and it remains now, as it was then, a tangle of woods and marsh, holding back tons of water. But each step could lead to squelchy disaster. It was through this morass that we pursued the bullocks – my brothers and me, the youngest aged 8, and the tank of a man we called Dada. Patrick O'Regan, who grew up in Mawmore near Enniskean in West Cork, and was married to my mother, who went by the name of Mama.

They met when she was called Eileen Horgan at a dance in Inchigeela in the mid-sixties. They both had gone alone to the dance. In the black-and-white past, we don't really credit our parents with 'agency' sometimes, preferring to see them as passive subjects of some sort of stultifying, repressed country, but they knew how to go and try and find a spouse. I certainly never had the stones to go out by myself to meet someone. And they did it sober. While at the dance, my mother saw no one she liked the look of and was leaving when . . . my father, who was late to the dance, met her on the way out. Apparently he smiled at her as they passed and they stopped to talk and a couple of years later, after a ridiculously small number of meetings – it might have been as few as eight – they were married.

My mother was in that part of the world because she had cousins there. Her father, Conor Horgan, was born in Gougane Barra on a small farm in a house that, according to family lore, is on the same site as the interpretive centre of the picturesque forest park. And by interpretive centre, I mean the public toilets. Yes, my grandfather's birthplace is now a toilet. To explain, Gougane Barra is the source of the River Lee and also where St Finbarr had his monastery and apparently fought a serpent called Louie. Which seems a rather unusual name for a pagan serpent. I suspect, since it was an early Irish Christian search-and-replace origin story, Finbarr just shut down some fella called Louie's mushroom party. But then the victors beautifully illuminated the history. Or knew a fella who could. But the lake and cliffs and small church at Gougane Barra weren't always just a backdrop to a thousand weddings; it wasn't always larch and Sitka spruce and wide vistas of a valley. If you had your wedding there in my grandfather's day, the shirts and ties were being worn by oul' lads picking stones. On their farms. Because long before the forest park made it the end point of a million Cork primary-school tours, farmers lived there, my maternal grandfather among them.

In 1966 my father sold the farm he was born on so that it could find its true calling as a gravel pit and bought Dripsey. I say he bought Dripsey as if it were a colonial pile carved out of stolen rainforest. I mean he bought 42 acres of land between Dripsey cross and Dripsey village. The land was mostly between the Lane and the Mill Road. One day he packed a young family and some cows, calves and pigs into a car and trailer and moved over. (They made a few trips.) And twelve years later I joined the organization in a junior role.

It's a small farm, and if you had a small farm and you wanted to make proper money you needed to do one of a number of things. Get an off-farm job or raise children who would be lunatics for land and embark together on a lifetime of expansion and acquisition and worry.

My parents did none of those at the time. Mama stayed at home to mind us and hens and help Dada. Although my father briefly sold detergent door-to-door in the seventies (a Bold move, you could say) and did a bit of contracting for other farmers, he had enough to be doing on the farm. And they just weren't that into money (earning it or spending it) so there was no expansion outside the ditches. We tipped away. (Tipping away is an Irish euphemism that describes a level of activity that is constant and busy but is not driven by five-year plans or strategic growth envisioning. It's a cagey response to the question of how busy you are. Tipping away does not mean leaving a few bob in a restaurant in Spain or regularly dumping rubbish in a scenic area.)

With the scale of the farm and the tipping-away level of activity, it was clear there wasn't much of a living to be had out of the place for another family, so we would need schooling. Dada did a lot of the farming by himself while we were 'at the books'. He wasn't resentful of this. There was no muttering in the rain about soft sons while wrestling furze. He liked books, too, and learning. The newspapers were piled high in the kitchen. The workshop outside had a filing cabinet that – as well as milk cheques – held numerous books on the origins of placenames and local histories about The Way We Were and What the IRA Did Nearby. When he came across a new word in the paper, it delighted him and he cemented it in his brain after looking it up in his Virtue's English Dictionary. So we weren't hauled out from our studies and thrown into a shed to castrate a load of disgruntled grunting bulls, our book-learning smashed into the dung symbolically. He did most of the work himself without complaining and called on us to help out at key moments like planting and harvesting and cutting thistles, whitewashing, painting gates, picking stones – the glamour jobs.

He would remind us of singular feats of farming when the family was young. He said he brought in 1,700 bales of straw alone in one harvest. For the non-baling aficionados, the whole point of bringing in bales is to have one small child up high on the precarious load on the back of a trailer, stacking bales row by row, each row at right angles as they fly up from the arms or the pike of the farmer on the ground. Then you get to sit on the load of bales all the way home, and hopefully it travels along the country lanes so you can act like a soldier returning with the spoils of war and play Avoid the Overhanging Tree Branch. But throwing the bales up and then climbing up to make the load? That is like driving a train while laying track.

It was a reasonably self-sufficient kind of life, once you count EEC farm support money as a wage. We drank our own milk – sorry, I mean our own cows' milk, this isn't Goop – sometimes ate one of the animals, grew spuds, turnips. Mama made brown bread and apple tart. The rest of our diet – 80 per cent composed of cheese singles, white sliced pan, Tanora, sucky sweets and sausages – was bought in the weekly trip to L&N in Ballincollig. (L&N (London and Newcastle) was a supermarket chain that spent thirty years in Ireland before being bought by SuperValu. Barcode nerds will tell you the Ballincollig L&N had the first barcode scanner in the country.)

By any standards, I wasn't much of a farmer. I don't mean that I left gates open or borrowed heavily to plant an unsuitable strain of cotton that failed and then gambled away my inheritance with a dissolute lifestyle in the pub, challenging men to fights and holding forth on a range of topics such as the situation in the Levant. I just mean I didn't have that pure hunger, that obsession that you need in farming. Road-safety issues notwithstanding, you needed to be the kind of child who would drive to your Junior Cert exam with a tractor and trailer, do English paper one, interpret what the poet meant about leaving rural Ireland behind for the lure of the city, bring 18 tons of silage to a pit and then come back for geography, where you answered questions on how the closeness of contours showed the steepness of hills, then speed back to the field to pick up a load from the harvester, taking care not to turn in the field if the contours were too close together. It's the hunger that requires you to start out with a small farm and, by contracting and leasing and working two days a day, build it up to a bigger farm with loads of debt and tractors.

But it's in me. Somewhere. You can know sweet FA about modern farming, but you can't unknow the farming upbringing. There's that vocabulary of words that you take for granted just knowing before you've barely made your communion: haggards, castration, insemination, spontaneous abortion, rotavating, nitrate ... Not to be all *Blade Runner*, but I've seen things you people wouldn't believe: bullocks shoulder a Ford Orion, calves scutter in the dark near the piggery gate. All these things will be lost like ears of grain (when the barley lodges).

These days, I'm a soft-handed city-dwelling writer fretting about climate change. So many layers away from where and how food is made and land is used. Buffeted like so many by a cascade of bad news and guilt, looking around for obvious villains, people to blame, trying to find the Duke Nukem type with the barrels of toxic sludge in the back of the van, asking stupid questions like, 'Hey, rural dwellers, why don't you commute by bicycle to work from your home in the country along dark lanes that you're sharing with lorries?' 'Hey, farmers, what's with all the nitrogen? I read something about dung beetles on the internet. Have you looked at them?'

Dada was what would be described as a 'tasty farmer'. The gates were painted; the pillars were whitewashed. He was partial to the Gramoxone to get moss out of yards; he dug drainage dykes in boggy ground and sprayed rushes; he hired another tasty man with a digger to bulldoze ditches to open out pokey fields. He burned back furze to make more land for grass. I thoroughly endorsed all of this for nearly all my life. There was nothing lovelier than sweet grass growing where prickly furze and briars used to be. And this was when I was 12 and obsessed with maps showing how many Waleses of rainforest were being slashed and burned in the Amazon. And my father was planting trees to replace the dead elm. So I knew he was one of the good guys. He loved nature. We would go on spins to look at solstice sunsets and interesting trees. He loved burning rubbish. So did I. On a Friday night he would look at the weather forecast, and if it was favourable, he'd announce with satisfaction, 'A grand day for burning rubbish.' Forget watching *He-Man and the Masters of the Universe* on TV.

Burning rubbish was the only place to be for a small child on a Saturday morning. The week's newspapers, bean cans, any plastic bags over the 8,000 we had stored just in case, fertilizer bags, silage plastic. Just a man and his youngest son, poking at embers in November fog with metal sticks. Then the EU came along with their satellites and RUINED IT, spying on the ordinary dacent man out minding, or rather burning, his own business.

I think about Dada and being wrong, being okay with it, trying again, getting it wrong again and carrying on. Dada and I had views about some things that time and new knowledge have weathered away to wrongness. About things like food and transport and energy and nature. Topics that have people at loggerheads. (As if the poor turtles didn't have enough to worry about.)

But Dada also took exactly six flights in his life; he and my mother spent their lives trying not waste petrol and heating oil, and held onto many things in case they came in handy; he pretty much chatted up strangers with the line 'Have a guess how much I paid for that coat in the charity shop?' He planted trees all over the townland. He quietly, gently was part of a community for which he did his bit by actions rather than talk. (Although he was well able to talk.)

There is a strong chance that you are currently feeling beaten up in your attempts to be less damaging environmentally and finding every step you take has unintended consequences. Or else the thing you've always done, how you make your living, has recently become bad. I know I feel this way. I'm trying to come to terms with wrongness, not knowing, thinking I was doing the right thing, then it turns out it was wrong, taking small steps, taking joy in taking them, informing myself, informing on myself, avoiding despair. It's not a book about how All Things Should Be Done. I don't know that I'd be able to squeeze into one handy-sized book a large review of the up-to-date findings on glyphosate, the complex calculations of methane emissions and their interplay with silage proteins, whether there's a future in the bacteria that digest plastic, the arcane twists and turns of the global carbon credits market, the interplay between peat bogs, wind farms, hen harriers, sphagnum moss, the question of whether capitalism itself is the problem and an actual revolution is necessary to completely change our trajectory.

You might need to read up on them separately. I recommend it. It's 100 per cent epic bantz.

And I'm not an expert – I'm probably not even a Good Enough Person. I'm not a spokesperson for ordinary people tired of being made to feel guilty by all these do-gooders, who are just trying to earn a pound note here and there. Sometimes I'm one of the do-gooders, sometimes I'm one of the do-nothings and sometimes I'm a do-badder. Sometimes I'm weak-willed or not aware of the newest research, flummoxed by conflicting evidence or locked into a lifestyle, a job, a way of life, a set of habits, a series of unfortunate events, trying to change some things that at the moment seem impossible or would cost a lot of money, and would it be okay if I sat this fight out? And then other times I'm up for it.

We're not consistent. Some people might appear ignorant about lots of things, may once have left bags of clothing at the bottle bank and bags of bottles near an area of outstanding natural beauty. But on the other hand, they may have never driven an engine larger than 1 litre, never unnecessarily attended a conference in Silicon Valley. Some people are burning gallons of diesel driving up and down mountains planting trees and saving curlews.

Because I grew up on a farm and now live in the city, crossing the rural–urban divide, doesn't mean I have a unique perspective. The city is full of us wistful types romanticizing a particular version of farming without depending on it for bread money. There are lots of types of farming other than the one I grew up with – everything from the huge operators with tractors that look like Transformers and sheds as big as townlands to the hardscrabble life of fields of rocks and eleven and a half months of storms and mountain sheep grazing, or the organic farms with the perfect balance between humanity and nature, with butterflies fluttering and Vivaldi playing. All I'm saying is there are bits about farming and the countryside and bits about city life that I *get*. And the balance between the two is hard to maintain for an average brain.

Speaking of the balance between humanity and nature, we return now to the chase for the bullocks.

We were obsessed – like Martin Sheen in *Apocalypse Now*. In the classic film Sheen's character, Captain Willard, follows Colonel Kurtz all the way into Cambodia. We were just heading for Aghabullogue. But we had to find those cattle before they went rogue and crowned themselves leaders of the native cattle. Bad things can happen in the forest at night. I was the youngest in the troop, just like

Laurence Fishburne. I stepped into a boghole. Water filled my wellingtons. I was stuck there. Any move could lead to catastrophe – as in, I could get soaked. I was losing my mind.

'Dada, come back!' But Dada ploughed on ahead, like Martin Sheen did when Lawrence Fishburne got water in *his* wellingtons.

'Come back, Dada, my feet are soaking,' I cried again. But he would not turn around. He was Captain Willard, controlled now by the obsessive need to bring the bullocks back – with extreme prejudice. I reacted like a true soldier – I started crying.

'Come back, will ya?! I hate you, I hate you. You bastard.'

But spurred on by the need to grow up, and perhaps to get closer to him so he could hear the names I was calling him, I pulled my feet out of the boghole and squelched on.

I had forgotten the trauma of this incident until one day I was reading one of Dada's old diaries and I saw the entry for that night: *The bullocks went wandering upriver. Boy doubted my ability as a parent.*

Never doubted you for a second, Dada. I'm too busy doubting myself.

The question now is – what to do about that doubt?

2.

Thought for food

'I know what I'll be having: the beef'

– Dada in every restaurant he was ever in

Dada was a beef man. And by that, I don't mean he wore a Stetson, helped pick Republican candidates and drove a jeep the size of an AT-AT to the chemist to buy his ninth gun. It's just that that's what he got when he was in a restaurant. The menu was unnecessary and only got a cursory look, like the guarantee on a promotional USB stick in a gift bag at a conference. The accompaniment to the beef would be spuds and then some sort of veg, cooked as veg was then to acceptably Irish levels of mush. Not like now where it is almost raw. The meal was predictable. Dada knew what was coming. You don't be blindsiding a beef man with an aubergine. You don't leave a courgette hiding on the plate beneath the mash. The beef was gone in a second. 'That was a grand bit of beef,' he said. He liked the ceremony as well. If the place was the right sort of place, an attentive waiter would appear at his shoulder with the two-spoon trick of dishing out carrots and peas while holding a tin tray. (I think the rise of carveries led to the demise of the two-spoon trick. Gone the way of whittling and black-smithing.) I never saw him complain about the beef – it can't have been good all the time. Or the gravy, which often looked phoned in. But then again, we were not people to complain in a restaurant. Weren't they making food for us?

The selection of roast beef was not because he and his generation were knee deep in bovine banquets all the time like ancient Gaelic kings. Rather it was because they were not. Roast beef was rare. In quantity, I mean, not the level of cooking (what – are you mad?).

We were all beef people. And for a while we used to eat our animals. Every year, for various reasons, an animal was selected, went off and, between the jigs and the reels (my euphemism for slaughtering and butchering), the chest freezer was full of meat for the best part of a year. One year the sacrificial bullock was an animal that had fallen off a cliff and broken its back. (Another surreal visit from a neigh-bour, saying, 'Your cow is sitting down in a ditch.' And he was, sitting in a way no bullock should as if in a *Far Side* cartoon.) He was dispatched – okay, killed – there and then by a vet and taken off to the butcher. Another year, it was the yearling with a hole in its side. (The yearling had a hole cut in its side to save it from dying from bloat – it wasn't a cow version of *The Girl With the Dragon Tattoo*.) At some point in the year, the freezer meat would run out and be supported by an increase in rashers, sausages and black pudding. This was before black pudding became the *Riverdance* of offal and celebrated in embassies. That old stuff was Wavin.

This background is not a roast boast. I'm not trying to set myself up as a manly red-blooded man who mans his way around a man's world taking bites out of animals like Homer Simpson in the Land of Chocolate. I'm not trying to 'own the vegans' and roar that I will have no truck with your leaves and that kale is for cattle. It's that I think a lot about meat now and there's a lot of talk about what all that meat eating means.

For me, life is very meaty. Not necessarily always good-quality meat. Just ever present. I'm not being played by Big Meat. It's not subtle advertising linking four-for-€1.35 sausage rolls to a successful lifestyle, me running for a train after knocking them back Berocca-style, that has me at the door of the deli like a pathetic lover coming back for more mistreatment. That urge to eat sausage rolls without a single shred of knowledge about what's in them, knowing they are filthy and they'll get all over my jumper and the library . . . I just eat them, feeling dirty and used but knowing I'll be back for more. That impulse comes from within and, most certainly, is not a desire to rub it in the eye of non-meat-arians. And I'm not unaware of where meat comes from.

Cruella de veal

In many ways, I'm a sentimental gobshite. I cry at elections in countries that have recently got rid of dictators, or when the plucky roller-hockey team win in a TV movie that I see the end of on the Hallmark channel on a hotel telly, or at a wounded crow limping across the road to the ditch, or when reading the last chapter of *Winnie-the-Pooh* when (spoiler alert) Christopher Robin is gently trying to tell Pooh about the end of childhood. I feel for inanimate objects. I salute a beloved pair of underpants reaching its end of life. I'm awful fond of cows, I call horses 'horsies' whether my children are nearby or not. I call puppy farmers the c-word in the Facebook comments under news stories about the mistreatment of puppies on puppy farms, set up to feed the Christmas market in presents for people with no impulse control.

But I (currently) also have no impulse control when it comes to meat. I know an animal has died for it. But that doesn't put me off. Somehow I've made the mental leap necessary to eat a thing I've seen being cute in videos on Facebook (a cow, pig or a lamb or a chicken, not a horse, puppies or people voting in elections. But the fact that I don't eat puppies or horses because it's abhorrent is another mental leap. Meanwhile, eating voters is illegal.)

I say 'somehow', but it's not a vague 'somehow'. That human beings eat meat while loving animals is a great conundrum and falls under a general umbrella of Weird Contradictory Shit We Do That Makes Some of Us a Bit Iffy About It and That Is Why I Drink. Scholars call it the meat paradox: the ability to gnaw a bone while our conscience gnaws away at us. Cognitive dissonance is a huge part of the meat paradox. Cognitive dissonance is a phrase I've seen written by smarter people than me many times in comment sections on websites and on social media – it generally means the discomfort we feel, but somehow get over, when we hold two conflicting beliefs. (Animals are lovely and some animals are yum.)

There are master's upon PhDs upon PDFs of research on the cognitive dissonance we experience about eating meat. The academics have studied us, and apparently we are an open book. And when I read even a smidge of it, I just sit there thinking, *Yes, that's me.*

There are triggers for the discomfort. It could be being reminded of where the food comes from. It could be accidentally getting stuck in a YouTube rabbit hole of abattoir footage, or reading the book *The Secret Life of Cows* and learning how cows grieve and have empathy and friendships. Now, even in the humane world of that book, the animals are killed afterwards, but the way they're treated makes me think about the animals that are treated far worse in their lives. You could be triggered by *exposure* to vegetarians and vegans. (Talking to them, not stripping.) In talking to people who don't eat meat, it becomes more obvious that *you* eat meat. And that can inspire a number of reactions, like guilt or getting cross about others' choices. Which is something I do *a lot.* I read about other people's efforts to cut back on plastic waste or meat or diesel and immediately think it's a dig at me. But my follow-up research suggests they are not aware of my presence and are – get this – *living their own lives.*

Anyway, the academics say that we tend to do certain things to make ourselves feel better if we feel this dissonance about wrapping our slavering jaws around a breakfast roll. Some people choose *engagement*. Engagement is another of those words that has been overused in the corporate world, chewed up like four-hour Hubba Bubba until it has no taste, but in this case it means they don't ignore the issue. They deal with the feeling head-on. For some, that means saying *fuckit* and ordering another breakfast roll. But others actually change their habits. Not many – although it's growing. About 4 per cent of the population of Ireland is vegan, with 8 per cent vegetarian. That's about 200,000 and 4000,000 respectively. That's a lot of people, so individually they can't be talking about it that much. But I'd wager it's still less than the number of people who don't kick dogs or who flinch when they see grainy footage of some bollox belting a cow being loaded onto a ship across the Mediterranean.

When you take out those groups, there's still a fair amount of us who just sort of . . . well, try not to think about it or come up with ways to justify what we do. The academics call them *strategies*, and even though you mightn't feel that strategic with a kebab in your hand at three in the morning, somewhere in your brain the strategy bit is working away. The kinds of things we do include denying that animals have the status not to be eaten – basically, saying they don't have a mind, or if they do they're not as clever as dogs or horses, or that they don't feel pain, they aren't individuals, they don't feel emotions, they don't have rights. It gets easier to say this if you think less about the animals and more about the meat.

The marketing of meat to us focuses on the farmer, who seems fairly sound and minds their animals, and then look at the beautiful cut of meat on a wooden chopping board. You don't see bolt guns and strung-up carcasses on signs above your head in the supermarket. The marketing material is light on words like rendering, boning and slaughtering. In fact, *slaughterhouse* has been replaced with *meat-packing*. Which is really just making your sandwiches for the trip. It's not hidden, but it's not on display either.

Lots of people who eat meat know exactly where it came from and are not that distanced from it for different reasons. Some of them are farmers, some are butchers, some just know. Some make a lot of money out of meat. Some love their animals when alive and mind them and then sell them and, after all their work, still only make approximately the 1994 minimum hourly wage.

I knew the cattle on our farm. Not by name, but at least by personality. And I herded cattle onto lorries. I knew they weren't going to Mosney. But I've never been to a slaughterhouse, never in real life watched or smelled or heard what happens inside. I've seen videos on YouTube, but that's not going to do much apart from make my recommended videos a curious mix of left- and right-wing activism. Though it at least makes me more aware of the pact I make in my own brain. *Here's what meat means.*

I feel I'm *meant* to eat the meat. Cattle are dotes but they didn't invent phones. Surely I'm above them in some sort of hierarchy? And don't I have these incisors – they weren't built for soup? And aren't the cattle having a grand life swishing away butterflies with their tails next to the ditch without worrying about lynxes? But still that whisper is there: *you know you're eating animals, don't you, Colm?* Animals that might have a sense of suffering or being parents or loneliness or fear or stress, and you don't want to look them in the eye, really. And no matter how many times I tell myself, 'Well, as long as they are treated okay', there's a chance that I am eating unhappy animals. Obviously they're fine here, in innocent, green, happy-go-lucky Ireland. But what about in Foreign? Will the burgers I eat in Lanzarote have led fulfilling lives? Look, let's not think about it.

If you too find that these mental gymnastics pull muscles in your brain, at least console yourself that you are not alone – it goes back quite a while in our history. The Greeks called it *akrasia*. Aristotle, in Book 7 of the *Nicomachean Ethics* (the best season of *N.E.* in my view), said akrasia is a lack of self-restraint, which means we know the right thing and do the opposite anyway. It's caused by 'the overpowering of reason by desire among the young and the effeminacy of some women and womanly men'. Okaaayyy ... yeah, Aristotle, thanks for coming into the office – sooooo, we had a look at your tweets and, if it's all right with you, we're going to hold back on you becoming a brand ambassador. So far, so very Greek, but it was all very well for the Greeks – they had easier access to olives. But don't get me started on olives.

And then there's the health side of it. Red meat kept turning up in studies. Too much processed red meat can be bad for you. But I was happy enough to shrug that off. Once butter became okay again, and That Oul' Spread Shite was found to be not much better, I went into middle-aged dad mode and just said bollox to any more reports or studies. At this stage if you released a report saying you couldn't put asbestos on your sliced pan, people would say, 'I'm not listening to any of them studies,' and be up on the roof getting old tiles for the dinner. So, I know animals die, I hope it's not too cruel and I hope they lived good lives. But I still eat meat. That may change but right now it seems the cognitive dissonance is working okay.

Don't mind them studies

But then there was another report. And it wasn't about health or animal welfare. The EAT-Lancet from 2019. A lancet is a small needle for taking blood samples. And indeed, when I saw the story, I thought, *Pricks*. It said that from a climate-change point of view, if we as consumers wanted to do one thing that would help – especially in the West – we needed to reduce our red meat consumption by as much as 90 per cent. NINETY PER CENT. TEN PER CENT LEFT. You'd basically be getting half a meatball a week. It wouldn't feed a toddler after a trip to IKEA.

Well, fuck climate change anyway. While the meat conundrum was just about animal rights I could resolve it internally with good old-fashioned guilt, defiance, pretence, denial and hypocrisy, and liking and needing meat is a handy way to get the protein necessary to support the brain function required to do all these mental gymnastics.

It was a personal choice. The health studies could be contradictory. But when it became about climate change, about *physics and chemistry*, it became different.

I had never really thought about beef and climate change much. Sure, we were told about evil ranchers in the Amazon cutting down rainforest with jaguars slinking away, indigenous people being attacked by rapacious cattle men who were probably conquistadorish.

But that was out foreign. Not our cattle. They're in an ad for milk, nuzzling a farmer's leg. I can't claim complete ignorance, though. We were told about methane yonks ago. But for years the story was that it was cows' *farts* that harmed the climate. And once you say 'farts', everyone becomes 7 years of age again and no one gets any work done. Even though it wasn't farts – ruminating was doing most of the damage. But according to Newton's First Law of Physical Humour, farts are funnier than belches. And a fart is an act of rebellion. That's my theory for why we didn't take it seriously enough.

Internal beefs

I like eating meat, and I like farms, farming and most farmers. So when I'm told that eating meat is causing climate change, my brain just dissolves into a mess of denial, guilt, wanting everything to be okay, and wanting there to be some magic solution so everyone gets what they want. But there's also a little voice that says, *So you're just going to ignore this: pretend everything is fine. Maybe it doesn't apply to us . . .*

Yeah, like, there's meat and then there's meat. I'm sure they're thinking about America, aren't they? All the cows there eat grain that's practically dipped in diesel, and they stand around in yards in the desert waiting for the rodeo. It's not our cattle. Our cattle are happy out, eating grass, the furze in flower around them, butterflies on their noses. And bovine herbivores are native to Europe so a bit of grazing is part of the ecosystem – their dung is good for soil and their hoofprints can make little habitats. And anyway, I read somewhere that methane thing isn't all it's cracked up to be. It only stays in the atmosphere for a few years, doesn't it? And wasn't there some talk that the way they were counting it wasn't right or something? Didn't I read a thing written by a fella who's big into methane and, like, I know he's funded by the American beef industry, but still ... I read that beef industry experts reckon that the methane cows produce is neutral because it's not increasing, and if you cut the numbers to reduce the methane you're only making farmers pay for someone else's methane and they're trying to get seaweed to fix that anyway. They're going to put it in additives in their feed. It's a bit like Gaviscon for cows. And the cows aren't the worst of the methane: it's the coal and the gas and the food waste and ... And if you don't eat beef and lamb, what are you going to eat – fish? There's none left, because we sold fishermen down the Swanee with the EU. And anyway how are we going to feed the world? Are you saying the Chinese shouldn't eat beef? That we've had all the fun and now, when they want to eat beef, we should say, No, you're not allowed – it's too late? And if we don't rear the meat, they'll do it in Brazil where they'll cut down the rainforests? And what do you suggest the farmers do instead – plant trees? And hope there's money there to mind them and that they'll be allowed to cut them down later for materials? And, oh, you want meat to be more expensive so we'll eat less of it, is it? So you're going to tell people on lower incomes they have to pay more for meat to force them to eat less of it and they need to find time to soak walnuts overnight or whatever you think we should be eating as protein instead? Wouldn't be surprised if this whole thing was a vegan black-ops. And what would your father think to see you giving *out about farming? The Common Agriculture Policy was good enough for you when they were keeping ye afloat . . .*

Now, it's not like that in my head all the time. I think about football and vigilante attacks against people who let their dogs shite on the footpath so it ends up on a child's buggy wheels and I turn up with nunchucks to bring the pain and say, *It's time to take out the trash* . . . Sorry – where was I? Yes, that mishmash of half-facts, conflicting views and conundrums does wash over me. So what I've started to do is, first, focus on what I'm fairly sure of and cobble together my own half-arsed, inconsistent, probably hypocritical approach. An approach that will do for a start.

So what do I think I know?

Cattle, for all their appeal, are, I've read, inefficient when it comes to energy. You get feck-all calories back compared to the calories the cow eats. The food mightn't come from a grain field. Some of it is 'free', from the grass – and therefore the sun, and the worms – but some of that needs help from fertilizer and that fertilizer needs natural gas to make it. Then you need to kill them and keep the meat cold until it gets to your gob. Smaller animals are more efficient. Chickens are very efficient. Eggs are better (though the poor battery hen . . . Jesus, the cruelty).

Plants, in theory, get their energy from the sun plus a bit of fertilizer and don't always need to be refrigerated (well, unless you're getting strawberries from New Zealand in February, and that's a different story).

Meat gives you higher quality protein, so you couldn't just be replacing it with Weetabix. Animals are good at eating

Thought for food | 31

stuff we wouldn't touch with a barge pole and turning it into energy-dense protein. But they still waste energy along the way. Beef is practically a delicacy: you only get a small bit of protein compared to what the animal has to eat. And, again, chicken, eggs and milk give you way more protein compared to the protein needed to make it.

The reason I talk to myself about energy efficiency is that it appeals to my absolute inbuilt horror of waste. I'm not faking it or indulging in some sort of austerity porn. There's some sort of eighties frugality that's very hard to shake so, metaphorically and literally speaking, if someone has the heat on and the door open, I get hives. There's nothing I like better than trying to warm the kitchen from an open oven door after the dinner is made. Getting an extra errand done on the drive back from another job is almost arousing. I've been eating more meat as a forty-something with no need to grow apart from outward than I ever did as a scrawny teenager who slept for eleven hours and spent the other thirteen worrying whether The Girl liked me back. And I seemed to be getting enough food then. Dada got the biggest helping of meat, but he *was* the biggest and was out doing the work, and I wouldn't have minded a bit more, but I was fine. It's not like I remember to this day being very focused on making the steak last as long as the peas and the spuds. That is not something I remember very clearly *at all*. (For some reason, I barely saw a chicken for eating at home growing up, but then chicken fillet rolls weren't enshrined in the constitution until the nineties.)

Even with inflation going mad, meat is still cheaper compared to incomes than it used to be. It's too easy to eat way more meat. And quite often, like Dada, in a restaurant,

I would have had the beef. But even allowing for the highest quality sustainable production that we have in Ireland, my feeling is that meat is expensive energy and protein, and beef is the most expensive, so it makes sense to cut back.

And even with the methane and the nitrous oxide (cows' piss), no matter what accounting you do, it's coming out of them and increasing the greenhouse gases in the atmosphere, and if there were fewer animals there would be less methane. We have seven million cattle here and it's still going up, and my demand is part of the demand – I don't know what other way to put it. And I'm not sure about the seaweed to ease bloating. Maybe one day we'll have ads showing concerned cows offering their spouses seaweed Rennies and a scientific diagram showing us how it goes to work. My suspicion is that there'll be unintended consequences. Sometimes when we innovate to avoid a harder decision, we end up making shite of it. Seaweed becomes the magic bullet, and next thing we're ripping carbon-sequestering seaweed out of every bay, and twenty years later we're standing around scratching our heads, wondering what we've done. But, you'll be surprised to know, I am not a seaweed expert. This is not a self-kelp book.

But what about the farmers – what are they going to do? If everyone cuts back here and abroad, they'll go out of business, won't they? Who the fuck do I think I am with my gut biome feelings and my average interpretation of the news and methane accounting? I don't see farmers writing books recommending people not buy tickets to see me – yet. But at the very least, could we eat less meat and pay more per kilo and have more of that go to the farmer? I'm sure farmers feel they're getting sweet FA for their meat. I look at the footpath of steak I can get now for relatively little money and I'm pretty much over the thrill of getting as much as I want compared to growing up. I'd pay the same for half of it. A whole chicken that costs less than a share-pack of Maltesers – that can't be right. So smaller, better portions and pay more for them. We're all in agreement, so? But are you going to tell people struggling for a few bob, 'Sorry, the price went up,' or confiscate half their chicken?

And we're already *fierce* suspicious of reduced portions for the same price. It's a wonder there hasn't been a riot about what's happening to chocolate bars.

So, my only suggestion is honesty. Non-patronizing fearless messaging that says, *the farmer deserves to be paid X per cent more for their work, you'll be grand with X per cent less meat. You mightn't even need to replace the calories if you eat the good stuff rather than the processed stuff. And it will have this benefit for the planet.*

Am I an absolute eejit to hope for this?

But what about THE CHINESE COAL MINES? And shouldn't the Chinese get to eat meat? And shouldn't it be Ireland who grows it for them, with our nice grass? And if they do, what happens if it's the Brazilians instead of us feeding them? I don't know. I've no idea what meat the Chinese are going to eat. Let them do what they want. And I'm not going to lecture the Brazilians about carbon foot-prints when our footprint per capita is twice theirs and we've cut down our forests already. (Not just the English, by the way – most of the forest was gone before Walter Raleigh threw his coat on the ground.) But mainly, to return to the short answer, I don't know. For now, the choices of potentially 700 million people with their own agency and the farmers of another country with theirs are not influencing my choices. And that's where I start.

So after all that huffing, all I've come up with is eat less meat, eat better meat, support the systems that pay the farmer more for animal meat, support other farmers that grow plant proteins here rather than shipping them in from Peru. I don't understand enough about methane, carbon sequestration in pasture, the global food supply, what is the safe number of animals to be reared in one small country so that its waters aren't wall-to-wall nitrate and algae. That's it?! Colm eats less meat?! Of course that's not it. It's infinitely more complex than that. But that's just the debate on the inside of my head to figure out what *my* actions are. Because those who know very little should be honest about that. Yes, it's rife with 'A little knowledge is a dangerous thing', and I may be proved wrong. A hard-hitting study will turn up that says Why Legumes Are Problematic. But for now, I'm going with it. I won't take it personally if I'm told I'm wrong. I know my face will break out in an akrasia rash either way.

Before we get our heads melted completely can we, as they say in all the best marketing campaigns, shift the conversation? From 'STOP THAT!' to 'Maybe we could start this.'

And just before we shift the conversation, here's a quick word on tricky conversations.

Rared, well done?

'What bit of the pig is this?' asks the eldest out of the blue. Well, not out of the blue – she's eating a sausage which we have encouraged her to eat. Encouraged as in not presented any alternative.

'Eh . . .' It's a hard one to explain. I'm not sure if I want to get into the details of ground-up trimmings and collagen from animal skins to make the edible casing. Although it is sustainable packaging.

'All of the pig. It's good because it uses bits we don't normally eat.'

Depending on your outlook, the word *good* is doing a lot of heavy lifting here. She digests that, with ketchup, and we say no more. For now. It plays on my mind, though. I've read articles about how you should give your children the choice, that inflicting meat eating on children is like inducting them into a cult and not giving them meat is also like inducting them into a cult. So which cult is it to be? And what age for the induction?

Some days later I open it up again, like a gobshite. While she's colouring, I say to the eldest, 'You know that beef is a cow, don't you?'

'Yeah.' She continues colouring.

'And you know it's dead?'

'Yeah – why are you asking me this?'

'Eh, no, it's just that I was wondering if you knew about where meat comes from.'

'Yeah. I know it's dead.'

'Okay.' I start to tip-toe away.

'Is the animal dead anyway or was it killed?'

'Eh . . . killed.'

'Okay.'

'And how does that make you feel?'

'Sad. My friend is a vegetarian.'

I dare not ask any follow-up questions. For a parent, asking a child questions about stuff they actually will eat seems foolhardy. Particularly when you haven't worked out how to replace the protein if she decides she doesn't want to eat meat. It feels a bit like asking a taxman during an audit if they're sure they've checked everything. Eventually they're going to ask why – 'What are you asking me this for?' – and then you start blushing and before you know it they're digging around and you're on the defaulters' list in the newspaper next to a car dealership that swore they hadn't two pennies to rub together and ended up paying seven mil.

We have two children. The youngest is less sensitive. I wouldn't be surprised if she ends up working in a slaughterhouse. And with the coming apocalypses, I think general rendering skills might be useful. She is more finicky. We will not be asking her *any* questions about meat choices, or we'll be down to three things that she will eat.

Well, what can we have, so? A tub of heroes

Yes, that shift in conversation we talked about. For so much of this conversation about th'environment, the emphasis is on YOU CAN'T HAVE THAT, STOP THAT, NO, NO, YOU'RE NOT ALLOWED, I'M TELLING.

We should also be saying that there is a bit of joy in eating sustainably. Eating differently, not wasting, appreciating. Food is so much more than beefing. It's about identity and fun and memory and community and tradition. We focus a lot on *instead* and *substitute* but what about *as well*?

So let's start with lentils. I'm joking. I'm not going to start with lentils. They're second.

Not Peeling Very Well

Well, this shouldn't be hard. To convince us to eat more potatoes. It's too early to say whether the World Potato Congress held in June 2022 in Ireland had the same effect on our faith as the Eucharistic Congress, but there's no doubt we need it. Irish potato consumption has fallen by 40 per cent since the seventies. And apart from being, well, cultur- ally good for us, like speaking a bit of the Irish language and knowing the etiquette for rural road saluting, they're not too bad for the environment. They yield more calories per acre than rice and wheat, and the amount of teen- agers per acre that could be picking them is a huge boon for boyo diversity, and young wans too. They're not as good as fruit because you have to burn a bit of energy in cooking them, and digging them isn't exactly worm friendly, but the growing spud aerates the soil itself.

I feel a bit like I've left my roots – or rather my tubers – behind. I eat lots of potatoes but not the way I used to. Now they get thrown into the oven for a predefined period. It's a theme of our time-poor, multitask-obsessed lives that I can't devote the care needed to *watch them spuds like a hawk.* Spending time with them, asking them how they are – namely, boiling them.

It's not an easy relationship. Boiling potatoes is like living with a compulsive liar. You bring them to a boil: they are fine. You test them with a fork: it seems like they will take a good while yet. It's as if you are saying, 'Are you okay, potatoes? I just need to go and do a one-minute task?' And the potatoes are all, 'G'wan and do your job – we'll be AGES yet.' But when you come back they're an emotional, mushy wreck, out of their skins. Useless.

This is the kind of behaviour that has turned many people away from the potato.

People drifted towards pasta. No offence to pasta, but you can't eat it on its own for too long. Or not the pasta we get here anyway. Maybe you could with pasta freshly rolled by Mama Trattoria in the mountain-top village from the 1986 Kleenex ad.

You can't fry leftover pasta for breakfast with sausages and black pudding mixed in with beans (a dish known as 'filthy beans').

We have moved towards rice. And far be it from me to cast aspersions on the food that supplied the joules necessary to build most of the world's early civilizations, but I never stole a lump of rice from the pot just as it was finished boiling and disappeared to a corner to eat it snarling like a feral child.

The second-lowest acreage of potatoes in Ireland was in 2019. I've heard of lobby groups wanting to to launch a campaign to get millennials to eat more potatoes. So how do we convince the coming generations to eat them, and ones grown here? If climate change won't prompt them, we hit them where they care the most: nostalgia.

It doesn't have to be real nostalgia. Invented will do fine. A recent data analysis of social media showed that a staggering 98 per cent of Irish millennials claimed to have worked on the bog as children. But they didn't. I was there and I didn't see many pairs of skinny jeans. (Granted, I was only there the odd time – I was pure useless on the bog.) But nostalgia for bog-work is tainted with climate-change issues. Bogs sequester carbon and preserve biodiversity. There will come a time when to admit to spending summers cutting turf will be akin to wistfully remembering the Amazonian rainforests you burned with your Uncle João.

But the potato – that's a less problematic child-labour memory. When I was a teenager, the autumn mid-term break meant one thing only: spud-picking. Nowadays, most potatoes are picked by an App. But thirty years ago I was stooped over freshly turned soil, grabbing a British Queen and stuffing her unceremoniously into a bag, thirty bags to a crate, and paid £9 for a crate. This was when £9 was worth something and not just the cost of half a brunch. The drills were crowded with men, women and children stooping, filling, scuttling and smoking. Proper smoking – none of this vaping shite – the hard-core brands: Sweet Afton, Carrolls, Major and the odd Silk Cut for the kiddies.

On my first week as a spailpín, pickings were slim in the first couple of days, owing to the field being stony and grey, but by the middle of the week the land had improved and I was picking four crates a day. The owner told my father through his moustache, 'He's a good young fella to work.' There are no sweeter words. They're up there with 'Well, Colm, you've passed – you can apply for a full licence now', 'I do', and 'You can cut the cord'. Then, after a proper week's work, my body comfortably aching, I went to the local teenage disco that Saturday night. Maybe the serotonin-producing microbes from the soil made me look confident, but something convinced a girl to dance with me (i.e. shift) without having to do a second – and more pathetic – tour of the dance floor. It was fast becoming one of the best weeks of my life.

So let's get back to picking potatoes now that the turf will be justly transitioned. Otherwise children of the future won't be forced to listen to any stories of the benefits of hard work as they search for tubers in the cursed earth.

The pulse on my finger

I have no nostalgia for lentils and chickpeas but let's make a new history. It doesn't sound promising. Lentils have become a shorthand for the joylessness of eating something different. Generally associated with Tupperware. You're eating your chicken baguette with a mixture of taco sauce and garlic mayonnaise, the cheese slightly melting, tomato and more red onion than you asked for; meanwhile, No-Craic Noel is heating up something lentilly in the canteen microwave. Like all out-dated tropes, it's hard to grow past them.

They are, apparently, the top climate-friendly protein. Even looking at packets of them in the supermarket you know they must be fairly stacked. Bursting out of their tight T-shirts. A trillion of them for €1.84. They need a bit of steeping, though. Steeping puts people off a little, though. Unless it's to get stains out, they're going to say the time cost seems a bit steep. And lentils are ingrained in my psyche for the wrong reasons; I distrusted lentils before I met them.

I blame Cinderella. If you remember, her stepmother made it impossible for Cinderella to get to the ball by forcing her to take lentils out of the ashes first, knowing she wouldn't be able to do it in time. Deliberately making it hard, you see, so that she wouldn't succeed. The same principle holds if you're applying for government-funded grants. Cinderella gets the lentils out, but the impression left with me was that lentils were miserable and a bit ashy. I appreciate that Cinderella is an unlikely scapegoat for climate change, but I'm sure I'd have reduced my meat intake a lot earlier if fairytales had been more lentil-gentle.

Chickpeas: a staple food all over the world. But decades after they got here, comedians like me were still using them as a punchline to a joke about hipsters. (Not a funny joke – it's just that sometimes you have to think on your feet.) I think we now accept that hummus is actually nice, but still, it hasn't elevated chickpeas enough.

I think meat is lovely. And all you have to do is fry it. Non-meat proteins sometimes require expert knowledge and a whole press of small glass jars of powders from Surinam to get them going. But to get these tasty proteins a bit more centre stage, we need to stop saying *instead* and start talking about *as well*. Our stomachs have plenty of room.

You can save a bit of money by shnaking some lentils into the Bolognese. You won't even notice, apart from a bit of extra gas. And you can use the money saved to buy nicer mince.

And pulses in general. I used to hear bean stew and think *that's stew without meat*. I got over that. Black beans? Now? I'd eat them through a sock. The emotional heart of a burrito. I'd leave out the iffy meat from a burrito no problem as long as I knew black beans would be there.

And I'm eating a lot of this stuff anyway on the sly in take-aways. The lentils in the dhal, the chickpeas in chana masala. The shnakey vegetarian bit of the 34,000-calorie delivery I'd order on a whim on a Saturday night. I just need to start eating them sober now.

I'm not suggesting adding chickpeas and lentils into the breakfast rolls yet. That will require a referendum. But let's start with another sacred cow, or mainly pig: the hotel buffet breakfast. How about sliding in a bit of dirty dhal and chana masala next to the hash browns? Don't say a word. Just associate lentils and chickpeas with free food. On a hang-over. With tiny glasses of orange juice and conveyor-belt toast. Not instead: as well.

And if you're just not having the lentils and the chickpeas often grown abroad, surely you'll eat your peas. There's protein in them too. Farmers are already growing them to feed cattle and they get nitrogen out of the air and into the soil. They might throw a few in the pot for us. But we'll have to start eating our greens. Farmers who grow veg in this country are going out of business.

But when you change, someone is going to have to pay. Not just with money, but with time.

The tale of the kale and the turnip for sale

'Your food box is here, mister,' my wife's WhatsApp said.

Food box? Oh fuck. The food box. It arrived in Dublin when I was back in Dripsey on the farm with the children, stomping amongst the hogweed stalks, letting them breathe in the soil. Letting my wife breathe at home. Meanwhile, actual farmers had grown some food and delivered it after I'd ordered it as an experiment in paying farmers direct for their food.

The website called it, as Mrs Claus said to the husband on date night, a seasonal box. That meant there weren't going to be any Kenyan strawberries. But there was a turnip. And kale. Neither of which we'd cooked before.

The things that have to change may take money, time or more effort. Sometimes they take more effort because they are intrinsically harder to do or unfamiliar or require some skills. Sometimes they take more effort because, no matter how much you want things to be one way, *the whole system is geared towards doing it the other way*. It's hard to leave a shop without buying chocolate for yourself because the chocolate is next to the counter and looks like your debit card so you've bought it without knowing. That's the system.

But someone still has to do the work. For every person telling the world they're 'trying to do the right thing', there's a loved one who has to help them 'be the change they want to see'. Well, thankfully my wife was having none of that. 'Your kale, your call,' she said. (Well, she didn't say it as neatly as that. I coined that. That's what I get paid for.)

Kale is seasonal, so it wasn't shipped from anywhere, and it isn't refrigerated so in mid-December it was as sustainable as a thistle. Unfortunately, kale isn't exactly cake. We used to grow it for cattle. *Cows went mad for kale,* reads one of Dada's diary entries from the eighties. Kale is one of my earliest remembered farming words. Like molasses or scour or beastings. (Surely beastings is one of the most savage-looking words. It's colostrum: the first milk a calf drinks after birth that has all the good antibodies. It's mad how it came full circle years later when I was defrosting it for our babies from little packets my wife had filled. But I definitely called it colostrum then. You can't be talking to women about their beastings or you'd get a clatter of a breast pump across the side of the head.)

Anyway, you don't mess with kale – it's a forbidding, user-unfriendly dark green. I looked online to find out what to do with it. You can make kale crisps with it, but I felt like some of the carbon gains might be lost if I just roasted it in an electric oven. And kale crisps felt like a cop-out. I just fried it with enough other stuff to make me forget it was kale. A sort of stone soup (but with oil, chilli, garlic and walnuts). And . . . it was lovely. Very nice, in fact. And kale doesn't have that broccoli smell that creeps around the house and lodges its fart essence in the hall so the ESB man wonders who shat in the meter.

'Look at you,' Marie said. 'One meal in and now you're telling me about kale's lack of smell. I'm looking forward to you doing a bit more cooking.' So I had to make soup with the turnip. It brought me back to the good old days of turnips in a pile in the field on the farm, covered in straw to protect from frost but enough to see us through the winter. The turnip doesn't give up its wares lightly. 'C'mon and have a go at peeling me so, if you think you're hard enough,' it says. I did and was glad. But I'm looking forward to the summer seasonal food box. And we *have* to figure out a way of eating our local veg so that the farmers who grow it can stay in business. Because once they're gone we're even more dependent on another country to grow it and . . . well, you see what happens with oil and gas when mad fucks have a say in their production.

We bought meat online too, from a farmer–butcher. Imagine buying meat off the internet. It was *mighty*. So far we're terrible, irregular, undependable customers. The problem is it's dearer and it's just harder to pay more for a thing you know you can get cheaper. (I'll take my Nobel Prize for Economics now, thanks.) I need to start thinking of a meat hamper as being like the toiletries hamper in a raffle. A bit of luxury. And isn't it a lovely basket?

Polenta money and no sense

Vegans have been mentioned already when talking about reasons why we still eat, or have decided not to eat, meat. But the non-vegan's relationship with the vegan reminds me of a particular scene in the Marx Brothers' *Duck Soup*.

President of Freedonia Rufus Firefly (Groucho Marx) agrees to meet and shake hands with the ambassador of the rival Sylvania, with whom they are on the brink of war. While waiting, he imagines how he's going to shake hands but then worries about what would happen if the ambassador refused to shake his hand, and he gets more and more angry about this. When the ambassador arrives, he says, 'Oh, so you refuse to shake my hand, do you?' and slaps him in the face with his glove and they go to war.

I think it's the same with vegans. People get furious with imaginary vegans. I have friends who are vegans, and the only impact their veganity has had on me is that they have made really nice food for me and my family and I've found out that oat milk is actually not too bad in tea. (Eat the hell out of oats, by the way. Good for you, local, trendy and the *amount* of calories per package is redonkulous.)

Sometimes we're visiting them and we have to buy them something because you can't be arriving in with one arm as long as the other, especially when they're going to cook for us. We go to a shop big enough to have an Other Section and wince slightly at how expensive it is for unappetizing-looking things compared to how cheap the stuff is that we can get piped into the house. But they appreciate that you made the effort and thank you for the MDF-looking thing you bought them (a much nicer version of which they can make themselves). They appreciate that we showed empathy in understanding and didn't bring a dripping carcass just to make a point.

They're not constantly *talking* about being vegan. They just get on with it. And I'm going to make a gross generalization and say that probably most of the rest do too.

And chances are at this stage they know about avocados causing gang wars in Mexico and almonds causing drought in California. And judging by the sheer amount of people going on about avocados for a while, I don't think the avocado toast people were mainly vegan. I think they were having sneaky sausages as well.

People started going on about almonds a lot more when it became apparent they were a vegan alternative for milk. But I didn't hear anyone talking about almonds for the decades they were the staple of marzipan. No one went after Auntie Noreen about drought in the San Fernandino Valley when she was lashing out slices of cake covered in it after Christmas dinner. We move in crazes whether we are vegans or not. There is a scare or a buzz and millions change their tune. Remember when thousands of oul' lads flocked to Flora when they got The Scare (cholesterol, not pregnancy) and were told to stop putting half an inch of butter on the brown bread (before they got the all-clear from the doctor and butter got the all-clear from A New Study). But when food is grown through unjust systems vulnerable farmers get shat on. We've been doing it since the spice trade.

On the more benign end of things, vegetarians and vegans make good food in a different way and sausage roll fiends like me get to try new things too. Making space for them makes space for others. Just like properly designed cycling infrastructure can make space for pedestrians and people with extra mobility needs.

'Exposure' to vegan food at friends' houses got me to do something I've never done before: actually order the vegan option by choice. I know! It's like finding out I go to 'one of those clubs'. It started with polenta.

That doesn't sound promising. But it was the first vegan meal I'd ordered in my life when there was meat on the menu. Polenta cake. It sounds like a caricature of a vegan food. *How's your polenta cake, loser?* And the name itself sounds like a brand name given to a medical device to make it sound more like a dance. But it's plain as can be. It's just cornmeal. Crispy polenta cake, wild mushrooms, spinach (ah well, into each life a little rain must fall), sautéed baby bok choi, peppers, red onion, sundried tomato and red onion salsa. And the eldest child was getting a burger-meat-mush-and-breadcrumbs and potato-extract kids' menu, so I did have that safety net. But it was actually not bad at all.

That cookbook was right. Once you have salt, fat, acid, and heat, you'll eat anything. At some point it is just a sort of fried bread but, excuse me, if fried bread is not patriotic I don't know what is. And, yes, I do eat the children's meat leftovers. It's a good model. Meat is reduced, and there is no no-meat panic. And in a sign of further growth, I've since ordered the vegan option when there is no kids' burger to finish. Thank you, can I have my PhD now?

You'll eat it, and what's more you'll like it

*'Best-before date? Don't mind the best-before
date. They just put that on it to
cover themselves'*

– Dada and Mama, many times

About 490 million pints of milk poured down the drain.
That's the problem they're trying to fix. And finally a bit of
common sense has prevailed. When Morrisons supermarket
in the UK said they were going to do away with best-before
dates and just tell everyone to SNIFF THE MILK, people
of a certain outlook rejoiced. Men who leave comments
under YouTube videos of Johnny Cash lamenting the fact
that no one's making good music now were in their element,
all immediately transported back to a simpler time, a time
when you were told to scrape off the mouldy bit, stale bread
was for toasting and that 'those little lumps add flavour to
the milk'.

Fear of being seen to waste food, though, can lead to
hang-ups. Even now it stays with me, the compulsion to
leave a clean plate. If my wife and I are eating out, I'll finish
my course, of course, unless there's something drastically
wrong. Not being a glutton, my wife will occasionally push
her plate over for me to finish and I'll try to accommodate
because I don't want our household to be causing a scandal
in the restaurant. But if I can't finish her meal as well, I'll
push her plate back to her side, just so the waiting staff

know I was able to finish mine, thank you very much, and it was Miss Finicky opposite who let the side down.

As children, many of us were warned to clean our plates. There were two reasons, both driven by guilt – guilt being shown by scientists to be effective in 80 per cent of child-rearing situations.

The first reason was for the millions less fortunate.

'Eat up every bit of that now. If you were out in the Third World, you'd be glad of it.'

Years of missionary appeals, Lenten sacrifice and Bob Geldof appearances meant Irish children had a very strong sense of the Third World, so it was a resonant guilt trip to use.

We called it the Third World, which is a since discredited term, as we weren't to know at that stage the colonial roots of the exploitation, the debt and aid traps, the ongoing tax-trading. We had enough on our plates. Too much in fact.

I'm not sure if this was specific to Ireland (being a small country, we think everything is specific to us), but with a famine just a few generations before, the cultural gratitude for any food at all on the table seemed to be a strong force.

The second reason for plate cleaning was 'After all the trouble I went to to make it.'

So even if you didn't care about the Third World, you cared about your mother and eating to please her. We all like to please, and if you can please someone by finishing what's on the plate, then all the better.

Now throw in the other emotional burden – the carbon cost of food waste – and we've another reason to clean the plates.

But from the other side comes the worry that I'm eating too much. It's easy when you have children. Not only are you cleaning your own plate, you're the family pet for their leftovers as well. Especially as you enter the apprentice-oul'-lad years of your forties and start using the word *metabolism* a lot in polite conversation. Without really knowing how it works.

When it comes to what choosy children eat, all the advice is not to make a big deal about it. Or they'll get a 'complex'. You're told not to be on your knees in front of them reasoning with them about how they'll starve and won't grow up big and strong and how they'll need their strength to face the uncertain future caused by climate change caused by their contribution to food waste or their father's waist. You're *told* not to be loading all that onto them because they'll get a complex about food and it could lead to anxiety. Well, everything leads to anxiety now, so what's the difference?

Lily, our youngest, has an odd palate. She'll eat a small tomato like a sweet – a thing I didn't do until I was in my thirties. She'll eat raw carrots watching telly, which I won't do until 2026. But when it comes to protein it's a struggle. She loves spaghetti Bolognese, and we've been sneaking in a few bits of turkey, but that's as far as it goes. And as for lentils . . . It's all in the sauce.

But at least we can turn that hang-up into a pick-me-up. One of the major revolutions in thinking in the last few years was the realization that food waste is carbon emissions, and when you reduce it you reduce them. I now celebrate the *joy* of finishing leftovers. I have a general view that smugness is a good hormone – although it has a slight smell so it's best not to show it in public. Just be smug in private, smug in the fact that no one knows how smug you're being.

Smugness in this instance is a fridge full of Tupperware. A fridge that looks like someone suffered a bereavement in a TV show about a large Italian-American family.

The key to leftovers is to get the stuff out of the pot and into the containers quickly. I've tried wishful thinking, procrastination and finger pointing, but the only thing that works is . . . taking them out of the pots and putting them into the containers. And that's where I get another mental health boost. Play a game of Spatial Awareness: The Pot Edition. Run your seasoned eye over the food in the pot, select a container from the Tupperware drawer. (What?! Of COURSE I have a Tupperware drawer. You don't? Take some control of your life.) And then watch how well it fits! You are the Terminator. You did the calculations on a screen in your brain. Then at the other side, when you're hungry, just take everything out of the fridge and then, smugly of course, assemble a 'platter' of stuff that is so unrelated you can call yourself avant-garde. Fry a rasher and have it with olives. There's your child's leftover mashed potato – put it in a ramekin. The last three grapes. Half a banana. The last bit of cheese, grated along with your fingers onto a cracker with relish. The king of leftovers is the fried spud. *Fry* a spud and a whole new world is opened up. And do all of this standing up. You can't put on weight if you do it standing up. Or so I heard in the bike shed.

Leftovers are also great for overcoming Takeaways Comedown. Takeaways are another filthy affair. Most of the joy is in the anticipation. You look at your life partner, you realize you both have the same idea, and before long you are mauling your phone looking for a restaurant. But it's a fling, a no-strings-attached dalliance with a food that's good for a Friday night but no long-term relationship.

But after those initial mouthfuls you feel sated, and a slight anxiety can take over. The pizza's too big. You've barely made a dent in the korma. There were chips with everything in that meal and you worry you won't finish them. What about the Third World?

The clean plate and climate anxiety take over.

Don't let that spoil the experience.

For takeaways – *plan* for leftovers. Make them part of the story.

For Indian and Chinese takeaways, on that First Friday load up on the poppadoms and prawn crackers. They'll take most of the edge off. If truth be told, that's what you were looking forward to anyway. Then relax. And look around you. There's a week's dinner left (with fried spuds, obviously).

Pizza CAN BE REHEATED. I don't know where I picked up the urban myth that leftover pizza is somehow shameful. A sign of a life wasted. Just fry it on the pan the following morning and it is absolutely fine. Now the pizza has become a two-day affair. Practically a relationship.

And chipper chips, you can reheat them! What sacrilege is this? Chips are supposed to be ephemeral. The following day they are cold and wrinkled like abandoned fingers. But I'm here to tell you that your climate-change awakening starts with reheating chips for a few minutes in the oven and they are good as new. (Now, make sure you're cooking something else in the oven too.)

Of course, the whole fast-food industry is a problem in itself because of packaging, the meatiness of it and the shitness of a lot of that meat.

But let's start with the waste. Have them with kale. It's not like we're going to be growing our own chips. Are we?

Using up the allotted time

Not quite. But we have an allotment, me and my brother. We have it nearly ten years now, so the tool handles and the boots are nicely weathered.

As a farmer's sons, the weight of history is on our shoulders. Ideally, of course, we should be bringing in heavy tractors, knocking half the gateposts off, working until three in the morning before the weather breaks. I should get involved in a boundary dispute over a nice beech tree that is growing into My Field while my brother fills out applications for the CAP.

But, no, this is not farming. Yet. I make no claims for it. I wouldn't dare. It can be very annoying to full-timers when have-a-goers play at the thing you're doing for a living.

It's how I feel when some celeb tries out stand-up comedy just so they can get some media about it, they get a cushy gig, get a few hollow laughs and then shag off back to the main job.

So I'm no farmer, and my brother is the better allotmenter. But even if I'm just tipping away I'm outside and not checking my phone as much. That's a good place to be. A robin is there watching whenever I go, always expecting. Like a dog who's heard a crisp packet rustle. *Wouldja be digging, wouldja? Would there be worms going by any chance? Take your time now, don't mind me.* Three seconds later – *Are ya eating that worm, are ya?*

We won't win competitions for prize marrows, but crap horticulturist and all as I am, the satisfaction of growing *anything*. It's so good. So good for the senses. The pleasing PHHTOKK! sound a ready-to-pull rhubarb makes when it's pulled out of its shoulder socket. Or standing at the redcurrant bushes HORSING into the bitter berries. Picking stuff and eating it makes it even tastier. Even bits of twigs have gone into my gob. For a few minutes, my unfit frame and soft hands are those of a lean hunter-gatherer, grabbing a snack from nature's bounty before bending down and sifting antelope dung to see if its owner is near enough to make the hunt worth the calories.

Apparently, growing something is one of those sure-fire things you can do to increase happiness. Provided you've enough things that survive. Which we patently don't. Including the annual fee, seeds, tools and netting, the food costs more than the stuff you get in a shop in one of the swankier suburbs that's been rebranded as 'Grocer'.

Our food growing is sustainable in the environmental sense but obviously not in the commercial sense. But we don't care. It's a thing to do. A gym for developing the few muscles the lat-pulldown machine won't reach.

And one thing I am good at. The best bit – rotting! Not bready rot or chickeny rot. Nice rot. Eggshells and lettuce. Potato skins. The stuff a fella lands in in a film when a rubbish skip breaks his fall. The stuff that turns into humus, the earthy, wormy stuff. I am in love with a compost heap. I turned over a tank of the stuff this winter and it was an orgy of worms and wood lice. Like when Indiana Jones is knee deep in biodiversity in the Temple of Doom. It is brown money. Not everyone might have time and space for this so if the next few paragraphs annoy, look away now. But it is ludicrous we pay companies by the kilo to burn diesel to take away organic waste at its heaviest and then, if we want to grow food, we often buy manure in plastic bags. We should be demanding our local authorities give us a place to bring our eggshells and mandarins and gone-off broccoli we optimistically bought in a Seasonal Box. We are paying money to take money out of our houses when it could be making insects happy, growing plants. It just feels so right. Efficient. And there's less greenhouse gas methane from it as well. It's very slow magic. The oldest, most natural process in the world: time and microbes turning rubbish into good shite. Yes, there's a bit of ick. But I don't mind ick anymore. When you've any dealings with small children you get the ick taken out of you handy enough. If you've any space at all to grow a tomato or a strawberry surely The System can be tweaked so you can find somewhere to start the rot.

So having an allotment doesn't make me any kind of farmer. And funnily enough, it doesn't make me think, *modern farming is for the capitalists – what I am doing is noble.* On the contrary, growing any bit of food gives me a small reminder of how farming is always on. Nature is bountiful but the fucker is also trying to wreck your head with weather and slugs and pigeons. But the highs are still higher.

Which brings me to my general hand-wringing call to action. Why shouldn't growing food in cities, towns, villages, back yards in one of the most fertile countries in the world be as common as pucking a ball or sinking a pint? In fact, pint-sinking is entirely complementary to growing food. Why is it considered an affectation, exclusively for those in the know? Why isn't every patch of unused ground in an industrial estate not carved into plots? Why aren't the cities ringed with market gardens? Make the roughs of the golf courses more interesting. Grow half-time snacks behind the goals of the GAA pitches. Why aren't the public parks full of apple trees and fruit bushes? We should be out in the park on a sunny day, off our tits on ripe fruit, arguing with wasps. Historically councils haven't planted fruit trees because, and I've asked around about this, *'People would be climbing the trees and eating the apples.'* The perverts. And if they fell out of the tree or threw an apple at someone the council might be liable. Or people might slip on the fruit. Lookit, growing a bit of fruit in the park or food in the garden is not going to save the planet but a few people growing a few dinners a year, even more people grazing a few snacks off the trees, might be a good start towards not seeing food growing as an affectation. It connects us to the people who have to grow it for a living.

Are you finishing that?

So, after all that, I'm not even going to dream of telling you what you need to eat. That's on you. For such a straightforward concept – putting enough calories and protein into our bodies to keep us upright – what we choose to eat can be a minefield. Leaving aside what we actually want to eat, it's influenced by cost, time, space to make it, family, childhood, comfort, health, body-type, culture, identity. There's moralizing around food: sometimes diet and sustainability work together, sometimes they work against. Many people already have huge hang-ups about what they eat – adding more shame to the mix is no good to anyone.

That is not what I want to do. All I can say is that as an inconsistent hypocrite, thinking more about food has been a way into knowing more about the systems that make it impossible, expensive, time-consuming, a massive pain in the hole for you to eat a nice thing that doesn't kill an orangutan. What is the connection between my stomach and the planet? Sometimes I'm making shite out of the planet when I eat, spewing out the carbon, battering the biodiversity; sometimes I am a Child of the Forest, a First Man living in harmony with Gaia. Getting three days out of a takeaway korma is not enough. Having a bit of fried kale is not the be all and end all. But slowly I'm starting to see food for the trees, the carbon, the plastic, the waste, the exploitation. I see where we individually have some bit of clout and where we are helpless unless we talk to others. It's inconsistent; starting out, finding out, is all part of the journey. I don't understand the enormous scale and tiny intricacies of global food production, most people don't. But the journey to finding out more is interesting. And the journey is long whichever mode of transport I use.

3.

I get around

'Mind the revs now.
Ah, what are you revving it for?'

– Dada teaching me to drive

You say you want the revolutions . . .

Dada hated revs. The sound of others sending the rpm up past the bare minimum required was like the sound of a lawnmower in a dog's ear. I never saw a man want to get into fifth gear so quickly. Once the car got on the road and got any kind of momentum at all, he went up through the gears quicker than Jos Verstappen. As the car trundled down the hill, within a few hundred yards it was labouring under the expectation of accelerating but wondering where the hell was the torque.

He would also turn off the engine about a few hundred yards from home and let momentum carry the car to its final place.

This was before the Nanny State insisted a car needed to be on before the steering and the brakes would work properly.

To him, the revs must have been the engine screaming, but I think it also must have been the general obsession with not wasting petrol. And it stemmed from the oil shock.

The stories we tell over and over again sometimes inadvertently reveal a lot about our formative experiences. For example, if you have gained my trust, I will probably eventually tell you about my top five times where I got the runs and how disastrous consequences were avoided. What can I say? I've had a sheltered life.

My father talked a lot about inflation. Specifically, the price of Tanora. I think Tanora was a cipher for petrol. He remembered being able to buy a crate of Tanora for a few pennies a bottle. But then the oil crisis happened and that was the end of the cheap, tasty Tangerine-flavoured pop drink.

I say oil crisis. Dada called it 'when the Arabs kicked up'. A pithy summary of the complex interweaving of economics, geopolitics, the legacies of the Suez Crisis, the six-day war, the Cold War, the floating of the dollar, colonialism, exploitation.

The queues for petrol and the increase in the cost of fuel must have been quite a jolt for a father of (then) three young children on a small farm long before the EEC started handing out CAP money. So not wasting petrol became a defining characteristic of his. I'd say he'd have loved when Greta Thunberg went in a boat to the UN conference to avoid flying. Anything to avoid burning petrol. And handy enough for parking. If Dada met Greta, he'd tell her straight away about how the old cars would let you freewheel home no bother.

His hatred for revs meant his top speed was about forty miles per hour no matter what the road. One hand at 5.25 on the wheel, the other sort of hooked onto his jumper or the gearstick, as if 10 to 2 was too formal for the steering wheel of the car that knew him so well. The car was usually a Fiat Mirafiori so he was never going to floor it. The Mirafiori was a great way for a youngster to learn all the parts of a car, as each would break eventually. Usually on the way to the seaside. For at least a couple of years, in order to start the car in the mornings, my mother would turn the key and he would lift the bonnet and operate the choke manually on the engine, bypassing any controls, a bit like the cow with the hole in its side.

I think, having gone through the ages of impatience and fast, I'm now happy to turn into him. The roar of an engine holds no particular fascination for me, and it also turns out to be pretty bad for the environment.

Let's assume that most of us will be driving petrol and diesel cars for the next decade anyway. Well, at certain speeds on the motorway, slowing down a bit will save some fuel and also some emissions. I know it's hard to think about slowing down on the motorway. People my age and older can recall driving in a time before the motorway. Certain coastal city residents remember the order of every intervening town they were once stuck in on Friday and Sunday nights, like battles they fought in a long-forgotten war. We should have commemorations, wearing badges of the towns – Kill, Naas, Sallins, Newbridge, Kildare, Monasterevin, Portlaoise,

Ballybrittas, Mountrath, Castletown, Borris-in-Ossory, Roscrea, Moneygall, Toomevara, Nenagh, Birdhill, Enfield, Gorey, Arklow – a special seated area for the oldest veterans of Naas and Chapelizod. The residents of those towns had mixed feelings for the invading soldiers. They brought business, but you also couldn't cross the road for an hour and everywhere was painted in various oxides.

Then there was an armistice. We got our freedom. The freedom to do 120 kilometres per hour.

And now that we have our 120, to give it away voluntarily or speed limitarily seems like a waste. And what's more, it's not just the 120. Surveys show about half of us speed. Of course, not you – but, yeah, definitely them over there. I know – they're terrible, aren't they? Shur what good is it to be talking to some people? But if you're chatting to them tell them this. Speeding is not just about safety. If you slow down you'll burn less fuel. Wind drag increases in proportion to the square of the speed. If maths is not your bag, it's like saying when one thing goes up, the other thing goes WAY up. Now, you can't be crawling along the motorway like a protest and modern engines need a certain gallop to burn the fuel efficiently – the sweet spot is about 80km/h give or take a few km. Coincidentally close enough to what physicists call the Dada speed. You do have to accept the ego thing of being passed out, but that's just psychology. It doesn't really matter what speed you do anyway because there'll still be an Audi up your hole. The only time I definitely speed up is during the terrifying white-knuckle ride that is passing a truck in the rain in the dark, where you are convinced you're going to be crushed *Fast and Furious*-style against the barrier.

I've even passed those particularly shnakey speed vans that appear after the motorway, just where you're a bit late coming down off the high of 120 kilometres and they get us like fish in a barrel. But I was fine. I was being virtuous. I felt like driving past them twice just so they'd notice me and tell me I'm a great boy.

And it's not as loud when you slow down a bit, so it's not as tiring. And you'll only be about ten minutes later on a 200-kilometre journey. Which gives you more time to listen to this on audiobook, if that's how you got it. Wouldn't it be amazing if you got to listen to this very bit of the book because you were ten minutes late for that meeting? (A meeting that could have easily been an email.) Or the ferry you missed because you were nine minutes late, but let's not dwell on that. YOU SHOULD HAVE LEFT ON TIME. DON'T BOTHER BLAMING ME.

When I slow down, I also feel I'm channelling Dada. I catch myself saying, 'What hurry is that fella in now?' as people pass me, or 'And what good did that speeding do him now?' on those glorious occasions where I pass someone who had roared past me earlier stopped at a toll booth, while I slip by with my toll tag.

But should everyone have to slow down because I'm feeling maudlin? Do what you feel like, but what I like about slowing down is that compared to the other stuff we're warned about, this one is relatively easy. It is the omission of action, and unless my day is so tightly wound and controlled and programmed like an actor training for a part where their abs are part of the plot, there's probably space for me to take a few minutes longer of a drive. In Ireland no one expects you to be on time anyway.

It saves money. It saves tyre-wear. It saves fuel. And if you're burning less fuel, you're not only avoiding the emissions from burning it. You're also avoiding the emissions from digging it out of the ground and getting it here.

Faced with an endless list of don'ts and habits that are hard to keep and things you just have to do in your life that are unavoidable like Going to Visit Mam or, ya know, Doing My Job, a foothold, some sense of a scintilla of making a difference, can help. Especially when I often have a sense of futility, given how personal behaviour can only do so much. As I will say repeatedly in this book, it is not just about what you do yourself. You are operating in a giant system that is still geared towards burning things that came out of the ground and throwing away things and working your hole off to sustain a standard of living that is either basic or (and the importance of this can't be understated) roughly the same as your brother-in-law's.

And if/when electric cars are everywhere, it'll still be a good idea. Power will not be unlimited. There will still be fossil fuels knocking around. We are not harnessing ley lines. That shit will still cost. And if we're all burning . . . er . . . volts like we burned oil, then we won't have the whole country supplied by renewables any time soon.

It's not perfect, because driving slowly on the motorway is not the whole story. It's not much good when you're bumper to bumper on the inner relief road. I know when I drive my diesel, even on long journeys, I still have to go past my neighbours for a while and shove the various Noxious NOxes down their throats.

But that's a different story. So let's tell it.

The different story

You have to hand it to the internal combustion engine. I mean, like, the sheer miracle of it. That you would have an explosion (petrol) or hot air (diesel) that causes a small fire a few feet away from your toes and this hurls you through the air. The whole thing happens about twelve times a second. And the fuel for the fire came from algae compressed over hundreds of millions of years. And was sent over in ships the size of parishes. And wherever it was found would find itself being liberated in the name of democracy by Britain or America. Just so you can drive to the shop to get Johnny Onion Rings and a bag of cans because you had an awful goo on you for drink.

So, an electric car, that just sounds better, doesn't it? Where the internal combustion engine is a triumph of brute force and fire, the electric car is just a small bit of magic. Like some combination of enchanted amulets. You have a battery that stores the key to huge power, like the ark of the covenant, you pass the current through a magnet, and like magic the whole thing starts rotating 'fierce quick' and the car glides off like being in the future.

I mean, that just feels right, doesn't it? You're using the power of the universe to drive the car instead. But right now, it's still a dirty diesel car I'm driving. And I'm finding it very hard to give it up. I'm not saying it'll have to be ripped from my cold dead hands, but for someone who tuts at smokestacks abroad, I'm still apparently awful attached to keeping a fire burning while on the way to the WEEE centre.

I bought it second-hand, the newest car I'd ever bought. I love it. Because it has been with me and the family all through the girls' early years. It brought the youngest to Crumlin hospital when she got her heart fixed – you could say one of her fuel injectors was broken. A few years later, the car would show solidarity with Lily when it, too, needed its fuel injectors done.

You don't need to be a petrol head to have enormous fondness for your car. For many people it's the best room in their lives. It probably has the most comfortable seats. It doesn't help that I have an almost child-like attachment to inanimate objects, so that whenever I come back to the car, I think the fact that it is still there means it has been loyal to me. So I'm loyal to it. Which brings me to the next head-melt. Whether to go electric or not. I'm edging closer but I'm having those internal debates, like with the beef. To change to electric means sending a grand car to the scrap yard, which I hate the idea of. I do about 9,000 miles a year, mainly long journeys, but the worst bit of it is when I leave the house and spew piles of nitrogen-related shite into the air, increasing ground ozone and depleting atmospheric ozone. I feel sometimes like I'm shoving the exhaust pipe in our neighbours' windows. But the car works and if I sell it someone else will drive it and they might drive it on short journeys and be even worse than me. They'll be revving the shit out of it – I just know, the sound waking my father in his grave. I'm the best person to drive this car . . . just like Irish farmers are the best to grow beef. Oh wait. See how easy it is to find yourself discrediting your own arguments a few pages later? It's also stuck in my mind that a new electric car has a carbon cost and, depending on the electricity mix, doesn't break even for a few years. Now this argument is a bit weak and fossil fuel companies *love* to see it being made because they know all people need is a bit of doubt and they won't really bother to do the research. There are enough studies out there to suggest that electric cars are cleaner nearly everywhere in the world, unless they're making all the electricity out of turf. Or really coaly coal. And will only get cleaner unless Putin attacks all the windmills and solar farms. Which he totally could do.

Then I also need to get over second-hand information that second-hand electric cars aren't reliable and the batteries 'are shite'. I'm sure it happens from time to time but I unquestioningly place a lot of trust in engines that run on explosions and they've let me down before. Also I'm so used to shite phone batteries that I think I've become a little battery-sceptic. But the chip shortage has made the world get over its second-hand battery worries fairly lively.

And range anxiety doesn't bother me. I'm usually worrying about something along the road anyway. Range anxiety would just distract me from ruminating on something I said to someone thirteen years ago and whether they got the wrong end of the stick. And I love the idea that, one day, local sun and wind will be guaranteed to power my car. It's so efficient. There's no dependency on despots. The energy has travelled very little distance. It's so much less wasteful than digging up a thing and shipping it thousands of miles just to cause it to explode in my engine to move pistons up and down. And you know how I feel about waste.

I think underlying my reluctance is the feeling that the internal combustion engine has been around for so long but these electric cars are only new and there must be *something* we haven't thought of. Maybe it's the waste and destruction involved in the new technology. Aren't we're just replacing the pollution in our own place with probably starting some war in Mongolia or Bolivia where all the lithium is? Haven't we just moved resource curses to places less familiar to us?

So what am I going to do with this perfectly fine evil diesel car? For a start I'm going to ring the roadside rescue people because the diesel car I know and love has broken down on the side of the motorway and I'm alone here with two small children in the back.

Nothing like a car breaking down to break the bonds of loyalty. I wish the problem was something really dieselly. But it was the alternator. The thing that charges the battery by converting mechanical energy supplied by the engine into electric charge via a belt on a pulley. The most electric, school physics part of a diesel car. It ended up being towed to the nearest town, where it spent a week. A week without the car, if nothing else, breaks habits. Which forced me to briefly experience various aspects of transport that don't involve owning a car. Now, I'd better say it in case you hear it from someone else. I live where there is good public transport. I know your situation. There's one bus every full moon and it's timed to be completely out of sync with every single facet of your life and every time you get it it's full of wankers testing out all their ringtones and having all conversations on speaker. I know, I wouldn't *dare* lecture you on alternatives to the car you own. You deserve proper public transport into town. Anyway, the car was stuck in Templemore seeking alternator arrangements and once the tow company got us home, we needed to figure out how to be without a car. (No one had a spare car to lend us.)

First, we hired one. It's the deluxe option. What you'd do on *Succession*. I'd love to do it all the time. I can't be bothered with the overhead of owning a car. The waste of resources in getting someone to build a car just for me and it parked idle outside most of the time. Why not drive a new car whenever you want – that hopefully too many plebs haven't been in? Hiring a car used to be cheaper than artisan chips but renting even a Fiat Panda in Ireland now is more expensive than getting an actual Panda. We handed that lovely new car back fairly quickly. Next up I gave the car sharing a go. Now we're talking, sustainability wise. Twenty quid for a few hours and you drive around a little Hyundai iSomething that's been on the go for a few years and the world and his mother have been in. If sharing things with strangers during a pandemic is not your thing, you might balk. But I didn't care. The virus is airborne. Wipe the steering wheel and the gearstick, open a window and away you go. There's worse stuff on your own remote control. I loved the experience. A car you can open with your phone. You book it and then you go to a car – you can even ask for it to be unmarked – parked on the side of the street and unlock it with your phone. If you're nine years of age, like I am, you can pretend you have been instructed to go to the car over the phone by a man disguising his voice. *You will find the key in the glove compartment.* Make sure to circle the car and look around suspiciously to see if you've been tailed. Car sharing was my preview of what life might be like without a car. That sense of being adrift. Dependent. It was a little unsettling. It takes getting used to. It's my plan for when I'm in between cars. It's. . . fine. I still wanted my car back. To collect the car from the garage in Templemore that put the new alternator in, I cycled to the train and brought the bicycle on with me. At 43, the first time in my life I'd ever brought a bicycle on a train. It should be the most natural thing in the world for getting around the place, but again, habitual inertia stopped me. I wish I'd done it sooner. I got to put it in the mail van. It was brilliant. At my stop, I went into a windowless carriage and waited for the train to halt. Another unique experience. Like I was being smuggled into enemy territory by the partisans, waiting for a moment to jump out before the soldiers came. Then I cycled the rest of the way to Templemore. I got some funny looks. Like I was on a horse. You don't see many grown men who are not tourists cycling around a small town in winter. Unless your local nickname is Mick The Bike. After paying for the new alternator, I got my own car back. There was a brief awkwardness when I sat in, but we're fine now.

* * *

So here's what I'm going to do: I am a diesel car driver who needs to stop but can't afford to be getting rid of a good car. Yet. The one I have, while it stays functioning, is free-ish. An electric will cost money. Self-employment makes me fear new loans as much as I fear not being self-employed. But when the car I have becomes 'always giving trouble', the next one will be electric, be it buy/share/borrow. Or fuckit, an e-bike! In the meantime, out of deference to everyone's health around the place, I'm going to make a conscious effort to replace all short journeys with public transport or the bicycle. It's sometimes a pain in the hole, literally. But I know it's a direct benefit to the carbon and the neighbours' nitrogen dioxide levels. It mightn't work for you in your situation. But those who can, should. That means the children will have to walk 10 miles for no reason if necess – okay, I'm joking. There's no point in tokenistic displays of frugality. I'll save that for the next chapter.

I need to get back to Dada and wasting petrol. I need my own oil shock.

Do they pay tax, do they?

'It's the likes of them now give you a bad name.'

'I know, Dada, and if I tipped them 'tis I'm the bad fella.'

A typical couplet between my father and me as we were stuck behind a cyclist on the road to Ballincollig.

'Why can't they keep in?' I asked, my hands quivering on the 10 to 2, unsure what gear to be in.

'G'wan away and pass him there,' he said, and I did, the '89 Micra responding to my pressing on the pedal with all the urgency of someone asked to do something at a quarter to four on a Friday afternoon.

This is me learning to drive and terrified of cyclists. Bonding with my father over our disapproval of these sweaty men in their Sean Kelly peaked caps and PDM shirts – even though we had bonded a decade previously while cycling around Dripsey on Sunday spins.

Those were the days. My father in his Farah slacks and sandals with socks – this was when sandals without socks just meant German hippy with the jazz cigarettes – on a purple Raleigh. A reassuringly powerful big West Cork arse on the comfortable, squeaking saddle up ahead along the roads as we headed to Mullinahassig Waterfall or Bealnamarbh. Tootling along at *Darling Buds of May* pace. Me and Pop Larkin.

Spins on a Sunday was a thing we did. Small ones, 8 to 10 miles in waning light on roads that would shake your bones. Talking about the things a boy and his father should be talking about – untrimmed hedges, potholes, nice trees.

And yet on the road in a car, we both considered *other* cyclists to be a pain in our holes that should be keeping well in to the briars. You would think that lived experience breeds empathy, but humans seem to have a great capacity for quickly defining the 'outgroup'.

He stopped going for spins when the roads started getting busy and cars made less noise. And maybe I got too teen-agery and awkward looking to be putting myself on show. You'd forget because traffic seems like it was always bad, but it isn't that long ago when there were fewer cars on the road. Most households had one. Some had none. Few had two. And no one drove themselves to school unless they were a teacher.

But those few years of spins were brought back to me recently when I was teaching my own daughter to cycle. The moment when I let go of the bike for the first time and she pedalled away, *Chariots of Fire* playing in my head. And she squealing with the pure expression of new mastery. But what's more interesting is now, after the euphoria, when she's moved on to the blasé stage and she's enjoying talking and cycling, telling me about the process of learning – 'Do you know what, Daddy, it's all about balance' – and then moving onto small talk – 'But, Daddy, do you know if it's supposed to rain today?' I remember that. Once you learn that grown-up skill, suddenly you and your father are equals. Shooting the breeze. No one is looking for Taytos. It's just small talk.

And I want to bring her to more places. But it's a bit of a battleground out there. The roads seem not only busier but also crosser than I remember growing up.

Whether it's two years of pandemic, more and bigger cars on the road or approximately forever's worth of pre-existing attitudes, it can be an angry place out there for all road users, so this is my tiny attempt to See It From a Few Points of View. And it will probably piss off every group. But there might be something in it you don't know.

Let's start with cyclists, just to get the blood pumping nicely. I am one. And I also drive. In fact, most adult cyclists are also motorists. On the other hand, a much smaller percentage of motorists are also cyclists. So there might be a few things you motorists don't know about cyclists.

- We're not slowing you down. In the countryside, maybe by a couple of minutes before you find a safe place to pass. In the city, not at all. We'll pass you out at the next lights. Because we more than likely also drive, if we weren't cycling *we'd be in a fucking car in your way, and taking your parking space too.*

- We're human and we break easily. This might seem obvious, and you'll be very aware of our brittle, bloody, shitty bodies if you knock us down. But years of click-/ listen-/text-bait media have helped to make cyclists seem like weird wheeled centaurs who are indistinguishable from the machines they are on.

- Do we seem cross? IT'S BECAUSE WE'RE AFRAID YOU'LL KILL US. DOES THAT SEEM REASONABLE? Most of us have had a situation where we have experienced actual physical pain because of what someone in a bigger vehicle has done. So when a thing happens, we often react quite quickly. And maybe what appears to be disproportionately. We might be a bit of a dick and swear at you and make you feel emotionally bad in some way. But very likely not actual pain.

- Since we more than likely drive as well and pay income tax, we HAVE paid for the fucking road. And anyway, there is no road tax. It's a tax on your engine. Most of us have, at best, a small battery.

- We're slightly high all the time. From exercise. So that's why when you nearly hit us, we might explode in a slightly incoherent flurry of swearing and arm waving. That's endorphins.

- This might surprise you: there is officially no hierarchy on the road. The size and/or speed of your vehicle doesn't confer any extra rights. I've checked the whole constitution. The only hierarchy is Ambulance, Animals, Silage, The Rest.

- We can cycle two abreast. Rather than two in single file. This might seem like we're just doing it to chat and, specifically, to talk about you. We're not. When you pass two abreast you pull wider but the passing distance is shorter. If you can't pass two of us safely you probably couldn't pass one of us either.

- Your passenger window is a lot nearer to us than you think. When we were all learning to drive, there probably weren't too many cyclists during the lesson or the test. All you had to do was not clip something. Parking, driving near a ditch – you don't need the leeway. You do with us. Not because we're hammered and liable to go all over the place (most of us). But because we're generally cycling in a fucking drain or a pedestrian is dozing, and we also have to assume someone's going to open a car door in front of us.

- Helmets are not like a vaccine. A cyclist wearing a helmet doesn't protect you. So it's really none of your business whether cyclists wear one or not. I wear one in case a pothole knocks me off and I hit the ground. But if you hit me, I might as well be wearing a tea cosy. So leave the helmet decision to us. It's one less thing for you to get cross about.

- If you hit us, you'll hurt or kill us. You might be A Good Person. But if you don't give us the space and attention we're entitled to, you might do a thing that will haunt you. We'll be grand. We'll be dead. But you'll be stuck thinking about it and there'll be no radio phone-in show looking for your views on Bloody Cyclists then.

- We're not as smug as you think we are. Mainly it's just feeling in control. We have a good idea when we are going to arrive at our destination. It's distance divided by our body's ability, give or take a bit of wind (of all types). Google Maps doesn't update us with 'Well, actually, it'll take a bit longer now' because a truck shed its load in a tunnel.

- And PLEASE, as a pedestrian or cyclist on a country road: SLOW THE FUCK DOWN. I'm just around the corner and you won't be able to see me in time. And whoever is in charge of the speed limits, THAT ROAD IS NEVER AN 80. IT'S A 30.

Typical holier-than-thou, zero-craic cyclists. Not willing to give an inch. Think they own the road. Well, okay. Here's some stuff cyclists need to know about us motorists. Cyclists, you're not saints. You could also do a bit without giving up any rights. Have a think about these.

- Motorists are human too. Separated from you, protected by the glass and steel, but still possibly someone having a shit morning. That shit morning is compounded by being trapped in traffic. So, if we ever do make an honest mistake, and you are shook but safe, take a small window before going nuts at our window.

- Honestly there are times when we can't see you. Especially if you're shooting up the left side, and you don't have lights. This isn't 'failure to pay due attention'. It's failure to distinguish a blurry black shape coming up towards us while a child is shouting in the back. It would be enormously helpful if you weren't wearing your Predator cloaking device. And generations of us learned fuck-all about cyclists in the driving test.

- We might not be in the car by choice. Our job may be so far from our house, our school choices limited by income/ underinvestment, our public transport, our ability to cycle limited by our ill health or someone else's ill health. Our choice of transport isn't *necessarily* a hostile statement about yours.

- Though we are driving through a cyclable area, it doesn't mean we started out there. We might be living in a place with no other option or what we do simply can't be achieved on a bike. Sure, let us know about the options for different use but, you know, don't be a dick about it and start assuming shit.

- Our bodyweight is not a character flaw or moral failing and is immaterial to the current road-related argument. (Although our vehicle weight might be if we're clearly driving a Range Rover for no other reason than *'it's nice to drive a tank when you're doing the Big Shop'*.)

- Many of us stopped cycling years ago and feel guilty about it. Cycling is like leaving your door open at night, borrowing a cup of sugar and letting the village rear your child. I used to be wistful about it. And wist is no use.

There was inertia to overcome before I finally got back on the bike about fifteen years ago.

- We are targeted by about a century of marketing and culture that places the car firmly as the default road user, an expression of freedom and power and independence. Bicycles have been represented as not real things. People falling off bicycles are funny (a distracted policeman in a Carry-On film), and they probably had it coming. The silly-billies.

- We are very jealous of your ability to sail past us. A lot of us would like to join you, but just now is not a good time.

- Motorists are probably consuming media as we speak that is soaked in car advertising. Or a talk-radio show that says, 'Coming up next: road wars – the new cycle lanes and the battle for the streets.' There's nothing sponsored by a bike company.

- The red lights. Jesus, the lights. It drives us mad. As a cyclist I'm always at the lights so I see everyone. Motorists crash lights. Cyclists crash lights. A cyclist half-walking through when the coast is clear – I don't have a problem with that. But going through a pedestrian light at top speed while pedestrians are crossing? Just stop it. You're being a wanker. It's corrosive. There's a spectrum of light-breaking but at least don't take the piss.

- This one will definitely get me kicked out of the cycling fraternity, but here goes. If you get a chance to let a motorist turn right and it doesn't cost too much momentum, do it. It's all about human connection. Give us a few right turns. Honestly, it's worth it. For a small bit of momentum-sacrifice on your behalf, by waving me across, you are contributing a lot to the karma pool.

- Let's say I'm driving a heavy yoke pulling a heavy load on a country road and not going that fast and you're trying to beat some arbitrary Strava metric on a Strava record and you pass me out, fair enough. But on the next hill up, please let me pass. Trucks and tractors will need momentum sometimes just like cyclists do.

- Van drivers – the oul' enemy. The stereotype of White Van Man is that he – sometimes she – is what is known as a Bit of a Bollox. And that's unfair. There are plenty who are not. And just think about one thing. There are a lot more van drivers now. Driving places they wouldn't have driven as much before and under ferocious time pressure. Why? Online shopping. And they're often transport workers without a union, forced into bogus self-employment. Late-stage capitalism is riding them raw. They are doing this to bring us all our stuff from Wish and Amazon and H&M. Possibly you met them the other day when they delivered the GoPro you're now recording their bad driving on. I've been in a row with one who went through a yield sign when I was on the bike. He did not look like a natural-born bollox. The front seat was full of parcels. He looked under stress. The solution to this is not you and him/her meeting and discovering that, despite your differences, you are both united by a love of dance. The van man/woman needs a proper contract and a union. A cycle lane won't fix that but just so you know.

- And a word from me as a pedestrian. I don't believe you're going to stop at the pedestrian lights. (I don't believe the motorist any more either, frankly.) I've seen too many of you skinny-framed (the bike) feckers tear through, so when I see you I get tense. Just do me a favour: if you're in that much of a hurry, at least put one foot on the ground and sort of scoot through the green-man bit. Then I'll know you know I'm there and won't wipe me out.

You'd be forgiven for reading this and wondering, *Why would you be bothered wading into rows between motorists and cyclists when there's natural gas leaking out of the oilfields causing so much carbon emissions that if we all gave up the car and walked everywhere hauling sledges till kingdom come we wouldn't make a blind bit of difference?*

It's because that argument is a colossal waste of time. Do I think the woman breaking her hole to deliver your new H&M jeans before she gets to her next job or the man on a bicycle bringing a child to creche are going to be the difference between ibexes frolicking in the newly unspoilt wilderness and lemurs howling at 50-degree heat? Not a hope in imminent hell.

So instead of wasting so much time on futile arguments, we need everyone talking constructively about how to share the road and mind the more vulnerable road users with as little loss of time or money as possible. If we're raging behind glass or shaking in fear at a near miss and then spending more time lambasting on social media, we're going to be in no fit state to give a shite about much else. And some things you can do nothing about. There isn't a nice way of travelling faster than on a horse and carrying all your stuff cheaply and in comfort. Until we figure out solar cars or cells that take water vapour out of the air and spit out oxygen, there has to be some impact of being a human travelling faster than a cheetah. If it's fossil fuels, you burn them. You get all that power from millions of years of compression energy. If it's electric cars, you get that from electrons and magnets but also some rare earths mined shittily in faraway places. And plenty of metal either way.

Every second hurling abuse on the road and social media is such a pity. Over short distances, cycling is just magic! The magic of mechanics, invented by the Greeks. You push your puny little legs a bit and sometimes you go for ages. The energy for it *comes from inside your own body* (or if it's an electric bike, some of it comes from the plug at home), burning food that you've already paid the carbon cost on. And you get across most cities in the country in less than an hour. It takes up no space.

Yes, the whole system of everything is geared towards the car. And that is not any road user's fault. Everything is set up that way. In this country we ripped up an entire rail network and sold the iron and the land for tuppence ha'penny because the car had arrived. And cars are lovely. They're freedom, comfort, headspace, playing loud music and shouting it out the window in the middle of the night at a puzzled hedgehog as you drive past. No one's taking that away. But we can make some more room. And when you make room for bicycles, the same ethos makes room for people who use wheelchairs or buggies or mobility scooters or the hoverboards we were all promised. And something people don't talk about enough: there are many people who would struggle to walk but could travel miles on a bike.

I know most journeys still need a car in rural Ireland unless you want going to Tesco to be a 'quest'. But it's the millions of small journeys that could be nudged in another direction. And while we're at it, why not make it possible to commute to a rural town from 5 to 10 kilometres out, or even 20 with an electric bike? Not on the green way. *But on the road.*

There will always be arsehole cyclists trying to beat their personal bests on serene coastal paths and arsehole drivers punish-passing you (until they get caught, hopefully). But a bollox is just a bollox. They were going to be a bollox whatever they sat in or on.

Phew. I think we need a weekend away after that.

Flights are not fancy

This section is shorter. You might find it odd that I am not going to go on about air travel and flight shaming and how we can all play our part. For a start, after the nearly two and a half years everyone had up until early 2022, being stuck staring at cracks in the ceiling, I'm not going to be the one to tell you not to head on a stag night to Newcastle.

I really miss flying too. At the time of writing, I haven't been on a plane since January 2019. To give you an idea of how long ago that is, my youngest child at that stage was one year old. She's now a qualified electrician. I feel like I'm *owed* some carbon credits. I want all that flying has to offer. The person who only realizes how airport security works while at the metal detector. The panic at getting your stuff from the conveyor belt with no shoes on and a beltless trousers. The sense that anything is possible in airport shopping. Maybe I'll buy a pashmina, or a lot of different coloured USB chargers, or something to do with Rimmel. I never do, of course, but when I'm airside, in a parallel dimension, I believe I can fly.

I want to be slightly shocked by the cost of a sandwich and pay it without embarrassment, like I'm in a Michelin-starred restaurant and don't want to let the other diners know I'm sweating I won't have enough. I want to go to WHSmith to see if their chicken and stuffing sandwiches are different. (They're not. All chicken and stuffing sandwiches are made by the same company.)

I want to be on the plane to witness the confident spill-free pour of an Aer Lingus air steward as they slosh the orange juice from a carton into your glass.

I want to drink a 330ml can of Heineken with ice in a plastic glass and say, 'Fuckit, we're on our holidays.'

I'm not going to tell you not to go to Eurodisney. I want to go Eurodisney. It's hard to be telling us ordinary shmoes to restrict the bit of fun in our lives, the guaranteed sunshine holiday before the Mediterranean becomes unliveable, when you know it's only 1 per cent of flyers that cause half the emissions. You can do your bit but it will take a while before your sacrifice turns into fewer flights. Airlines flew empty planes, or near enough, in Europe during lockdowns just to keep their take-off slots. Other scuts were flying 40-tonne metal boxes in the sky *just to avoid refunds*. That's basically private-jet carry-on without the glamour. And the private jet industry is booming as well and ten times as bad per person for emissions. That's the kind of shit you're up against when wondering if it's right to go Torremolinos for a cheap glass of beer at eleven and send photos home of your toes.

Unlike driving, it's hard to make the link between your little trip and emissions. Look, wasn't the plane going anyway? But cheap flights and lots of people getting them means more planes so . . . I . . . I don't know how to sugar-coat it. It *is* you. But it's not you being a dick. It's just you wanting to go on holidays. That's not an unreasonable expectation. Living on a relatively affluent wet island, that you might want to get a plane to get off it the odd time. But yes, do your bit to cut back your personal flying. It's a good idea. But if you do have to fly, don't be feeling shame about it. Don't waste energy on that. The world needs your hope and your ideas and willingness to try new things. An often repeated point made by brainy people is that guilt and shame are two very different things. Guilt focuses on the behaviour; shame focuses on the self. If you're feeling ashamed, it can make you turn inwards and be less likely to change your behaviour because you, the person, are being condemned and your actions have become part of your identity and possibly a badge of honour.

Update: Since writing this we had one trip to London. And once I'd bought my first pashmina and spent three precautionary hours waiting for security to open, I'm not in a rush back on a plane. I'm a bit more open to a different way of travelling. The children are nearly at the age where the journey is part of the holiday. And if we have the money and the time, I'm generally going to spend most of my time in Ireland anyway. Because I want to get back on public transport. And *everything* it has to offer.

Bus move

My attitude to public transport here in Ireland has gone through a number of phases that might be familiar to other sometime users.

- Childhood: no choice but to use it.

- Have a choice: assume it's shite because I hear people complaining. Drive instead.

- Circumstances force me to use it and I discover it's better than I thought it was.

- Actively use it to avoid driving.

The railway map of Ireland looks like the government lost control of large stretches of the hinterland to rebels. It was nearly a century after the British left before we laid any new track. And I was once on a DART where the driver forgot to stop and had to walk through the carriages to reverse into the station. We like to take the piss out of our public transport. Especially if we have an option of not using it. Still, though, in the last few years I've started to say, 'Hey, Google Maps, how would we get there without a car?' And sure enough, there we are nipping from a bus to a tram to a DART and zipping round the city, getting nearly every-where we want to go, with happy children gawping out the top deck or out the window of the train at one of the world's nicest mid-level harbours and thinking, *Do you know what? People should get public transport more often. Why don't they?*

Because they may not live in a city, Colm. For the hell of it, why not go onto Google Maps and put in two Irish country towns and see how to get to them on public transport? See how much walking in the ditch you have to do?

Google Maps isn't going to tell you, 'To be honest, I'd get your mam to drive you,' or, 'Have you tried thumbing?' But it will tell you, 'If you leave now you'll be there in 40 minutes, but if you miss that bus it will take you 18 hours, as you'll have to spend a night with an innkeeper on the way.' I remember coming home to Dripsey a few years ago and asking my mother innocently about the late bus.

'Are you going out in town tonight?'

'I might do.'

'How are you getting home?'

'I'll get the late bus.'

'It's gone.'

'WHAT?!'

'Oh, that's gone with a good while.'

Bus Éireann route 233 from Cork to Macroom – specifically the 'via Coachford' variation – was as much a part of growing up as grey slacks and EasiSingles. And as time went on, the 10:30 p.m. departure would play an increasingly important part in my life. I was a wild teenager, often out in town on school nights. (Interschool debating competitions, if you must know. That old story of someone who fell in with the right crowd and started staying out late.) After a few 50p burgers in Mandy's, I would go to Parnell Place for the late bus home.

The late bus was the grown-up bus. There was no horde of school-jumpered adolescents swarming around the door to get the seats down the back. Other than the occasional mutterings of a passing 'quare-hawk' – a mysterious group believed by the mothers of the world to haunt the dark – the after-hours bus station was a more sedate place. You waited with the other People of the Night. You were part of an anonymous collective who remained tight-lipped about their reasons for being out late.

During college, the late bus often played another role. It was the red line between two versions of a night out. It was the pause button in a Drinkaware ad, the refusal of The One That's One Too Many. If I got it, it would be 40 minutes of excruciating bladder-related pain. But it was worth it. I got my heated-up dinner, a bed and breakfast the following day.

If missed the late bus the night could end with me shivering on the kitchen floor of some student gaff because there was nowhere else to sleep as someone was riding on the couch.

The late bus went 'all over the place' to gather up the waifs and strays of the night. After leaving the city, it went out the Lee Road, soaring high above the flood plain before sweeping down to the twisty bridge at Leemount. It paused briefly at the junction there. Those of us for whom the bladder pain had now spread to the lower back silently urged the driver to take the shortest route home. But instead, it doubled back towards the Carrigrohane Straight and into Ballincollig, where the passengers were complemented by The Man Who Wanted to Talk to the Driver.

This is a man that you never see in an ad for Bulmers Irish Cider. In fact, Bulmers ads are probably the most unrealistic portrayal of rural drinking you will ever see in your life: a crowd of people with good skin and hair congregating in a marquee on the edge of an orchard while Steve Earl sells out? *How are they all going to get home?* I wonder. *Is Bulmers going to lay on a fleet of minivans?*

The true image of rural drinking is a single man in his fifties, who lives somewhere between Inniscarra and Macroom, getting on the late bus in Ballincollig at closing time and chatting loudly to the driver about that 'bad bastard of a bend'.

The bus driver listened politely as the man in the front passenger seat gave his views on bus driving. And he dropped him right at the door of his house or at the end of his lane. And Paddy/Johnny/Micky – having suffered no inconvenience except for a rather unsteady descent of the steep steps of a Salvador Caetano Enigma coach – was safely home. What is his fate now? Who's bringing him home?

But The Man Who Wanted to Talk to the Driver and I were sometimes the only passengers after Ballincollig on a bus that had another 20 miles to go, so presumably the route was costing far too much per person. But these routes are not innovative zirconium-cell-fuelled anti-gravity cars or startups that can turn shite-talk into biomass. There's no light-rail, monorail or dado rail. They're boring, simple buses that travel from one place to another driven by the working man and woman for the working man and woman. Union jobs to move people between towns in the countryside. Buses that you might use to get home from the city after being out late enough to have a bit of fucking dessert with your dinner or see the band play their old stuff instead of having to rush for the Half-Nine.

Because when buses disappear you start to doubt the idea of public transport in the countryside. And it is better than I thought it was. We were in Cork city in the spring and thought about getting a bus. *I wonder does our Leap card work?* I thought. It did. It felt futuristic (even though it's worked for years) to have a joined-up transport card. But more interesting was that my expectations were so low – because of lack of use, the fact that complaints make the headlines, years of driving and the public transport network not always telling us about the new stuff they've put in. Even when electric cars come in, the most efficient way of travelling is in a big box with other people. But we have to demand, use, trust the network. Get all the buses put back. And people will get back on them, bladders bursting. But they'll get home. Schedule it and they'll come. It worked for the roads. When we built more of them and made those roads wider they all filled up. Induced demand, they call it. How about a few bus inductors?

4.

What's wrong with
the one you have?

> *Dada: 'Have a guess how much*
> *I gave for this jumper.'*
>
> *Me: [guessing too high]*
>
> *Dada: 'Two euro in Enable Ireland!*
> *Where would you be going?'*
>
> **– Dada any time we met after discovering a good**
> **charity shop.**

Dada died in 2015. These days we're getting around to sorting his photocopies of 'interesting clippings from newspapers' and soon we're going to have to reckon with the rest of Dada's clothes. The good clothes. The Wedding Suit. The sports jacket that he bought to look a bit like Jim Rockford of *The Rockford Files*. (Dada was a ringer for James Garner in my eyes anyway.) Not the duds. The duds were taken out a good while ago. Duds is what my mother calls the clothes you can't wait to get into after being out somewhere that requires nice clothes. I haven't heard it much since I left home. It's closer in meaning to the original Middle English *dudde* – worn-out or raggedy clothing. The relief of taking off nice clothes was always palpable. The stress of trying to keep them clean, not getting soup on them, was over. Once you were in your duds you wouldn't need to worry about where you sat or placed an elbow. You could even sit in Dada's Chair. (If he wasn't in it, of course. In a farmer's kitchen there will often be a chair that is the main farmer's, and you sit on it at your own risk. It is accepted that there may be various forms of earth, silage and waste oil on it.) It occurs to me that nearly all the clothes I own now could function as nice clothes.

Although I still have stains on everything. It's a mystery to me how people who do TV regularly can readily lay their hands on a jumper that doesn't have bits of toothpaste on it.

So the duds are gone. Clearing out clothing is part of the necessary, brutal tough love of emptying a house so that men can come and put up Gyproc to stop the damp on 150-year-old farmhouse walls. As well as the duds, there were a lot of shirts from the charity shops. Shirts with brand names that showed they were bought new by the original owner in The Menswear Shop in The Town for Nora and Larry's wedding. Faded wrinkly collars and the brand name in cursive script – *Thomas Bramwell of London* or somewhere else Carnaby Street-sounding. But the label says it's Fabriqué en Vietnam. When a parent dies it is the end of a benign regime. It's a cruel realization that not all the objects we are fond of will be similarly respected by the next generation. Things get thrown out that wouldn't have been countenanced at all under the old government.

'Hold onto that there – it might be handy for something,' Dada would say as he spotted something that was otherwise headed for the bin.

My parents (and me to a lesser extent) were not necessarily hoarders but they were less Marie Kondo and more Marie Kon-don't throw that away at all. Partly it was that when you have a farm which has outhouses, there is just more space, and therefore more time, to consider whether something has to be thrown away or not. Once you've made the decision you don't need something, inertia sets in. *I'll just put that over there for now.* We burned the household rubbish; some metal things were often hurled into a forgiving *Lonicera* hedge. Or taken to the scrap yard. But there was another category: the indescribable doodahs and gewgaws, the table-quiz trophies that now housed one particular type of rawl plug and swallow-fledgling droppings, a jumper that was bought for a confirmation now saturated in waste oil, a hot-water bottle that could be cut up for something. Items that worked their way progressively further and further away from the house, through the outhouses, until what was once a wedding present now had a hoofprint in it.

They were also people who had a terrible fondness for inanimate objects. 'That's a great oul' rollicker of a jumper,' my mother would say, the highest accolade for an item of clothing, a statement of its loyalty. My wife teases me about my attachment to the most worthless of objects. I think it's revenge for the time we were on holidays and her shoes gave out – legitimately unfixable, due diligence was done – and she left them in a bin and I kept making whimpering noises saying it was the shoes still waiting for us to come for them, until gradually their cries faded. 'Colm, *stoppit!*' she shouted, the guilt obviously getting to her. I was joking but ... actually I wasn't. Those shoes are probably still wondering where their feet went.

And my parents hated waste. Wasting food, petrol, money, stuff. It's not a moral judgement on anyone who does waste things – who am I kidding? Of course it is!

The idea of single use or broken and no attempt to repair or hand down to the next child. Of all the human things we do as humans being human, the whole system being set up to get us to buy, use and throw away things as the cleverest way we can think of to keep people in jobs seems the stupidest thing to do.

Now it absolutely must be said, I also think I've reached the natural age for moaning about waste, getting the use out of something until the bitter end, long after it's practical or economically viable, just to be able to pontificate to younger people on an important lesson about the value of things. This is my right. The payback from the universe when your body and mind plateau and start to decline, when you get to the stage where you don't think you can trust your hamstrings to support anything more than a brisk scuttle to stop a child jumping in front of a car and you can't remember what you came into the kitchen for. You are given licence to assume that the younger generation with their profligate fun-loving ways could learn a thing or two from you. This shit I can do in my sleep.

But also three important points:

- Turning away from Having More Stuff can be a relief.

- When you're as cool as me, it's hard to admit but . . . Stuff reduction is fun.

- It was people my age and older who did the damage, and we have to do something about it (see Chapter 6) and young people are already doing their bit.

Stuff retention issues

It's all very well for me to say Use Less Stuff. I cannot stress enough that *anyone* who suggests that others Use Less Stuff needs to be extremely careful they don't sound like 'Okay, sorry, Funland's actually closed. Yeah, I know I've been here for the last twenty years and am just a bit jaded with Funland, but it's closed now before *you* can have your fun. I've got my house/had a family/cut down all the trees/got all the Bluetooth earphones I need/eaten the meat/driven the car/flown the flights/made an eejit of myself trying to find a soulmate and found one, but unfortunately, now, you'll have to do things the hard way because the planet's in a mess that was caused before you were born or while you were poor.'

I don't know where you are in your Stuff Cycle. It might be quite a stuffy time for you, and there is nothing more annoying than blissfully ignorant smugness, so I'll just talk about me first. When I was younger I wasn't so second-handy and waste-conscious. I think maybe as a reaction to eighties and nineties Ireland, when I got a proper job I certainly wasn't keeping any worms and telling everyone about charity-shop deals. I was SICK of thrift and sparing the oil and shit clothes. It was Big Job Above in Dublin time. I had a job that I got because I had one of those degrees considered useful and because I answered questions in interviews like 'Are you a team player?' quite well. I was living full bore in the Celtic Tiger era, or at least within the limits of my genes. I worked abroad for a while and flew home every weekend. One night I bought a cocktail. Jumpers I never even wore (they somehow *still* got toothpaste on them). It was heady stuff. The classic tale of a culchie abroad in the Big Smoke letting the money go to his head. I could walk into any shop and get pretty much any bar of chocolate or crisps they had on offer there, even the artisan ones. I went skiing. I had the heat on and the windows open. I wanted money for status and stuff.

So I've had my fun. And I don't want to be telling anyone they can't have theirs.

But for the first time ever, could we possibly be at a stage where stuff is not important? Yes, for years self-help books and versions of organized religion have tried to tell us that the acquisition of possessions is ultimately meaningless, that you can't take it with you and on their deathbed no one talks about what they own or how much money they made. (We *think* that's what people don't talk about on their deathbeds. We only have their relatives' word for it and they could just be focusing on the will.)

But despite all that, the economy still depends on us measuring our self-worth by stuff – there was no persuasive reason not to before now. Well, there was but we weren't persuaded. Stuff needs someone (often someone who is paid very little) and energy to dig it, shape it, lug it and dispose of it. It has always been destructive, but most of that harm was done in Other Countries Far Away, not in our lucky country. Ones that maybe you gave money to for Lent. We didn't really question the Stuff System. But could selfishness motivate us? Now too much stuff and an economic system entirely contingent on constant consumption is going to make the place unliveable for OUR children TOO? With the world ending for *everyone* apart from those on the Spaceship, the Floating Island Far from Anywhere, or even, depending on how climate change works out, Fortress Ireland, the idea of aggressively chasing luxury stuff, status and stashing cash just seems . . . well, pointless.

That'd suit me fine. It's a great excuse not to buy stuff.

What if stuffism became anti-social? Imagine, just like that you could stop worrying. All your fancy stuff was just a sign that somewhere down the supply chain you are shitting on an otter. What if increased awareness meant you finally realized everything cheap is stealing from poor people or their environment elsewhere?

You don't even have to tell people. You just need to know inside and smile smugly to yourself as you reapply silage-wrapping patching tape to the bumper of your car in case it comes off on the motorway. (A very specific totally hypothetical situation.) I'd love it. Ostentatious thrift or stuff-neglect as a virtue? Perfect for anyone self-employed struggling to justify their career to their peers in safer jobs.

I can put all my dowdiness down to, not lack of success or money or being a tightarse, but to fighting the good fight. At one stroke a huge source of dissatisfaction gone.

I just need money for the mortgage, a few bills, some sort of stash of canned food for my old age in The After Times. We mightn't even need college funds for the two children. By that stage, the whole notion of career may have changed to one of Apprenticeships for Adaptation. They'll be out getting survivalist training.

Anyway the point is, stuff is nonsense. And no better man than me to espouse that attitude with open arms.

Getting myself fixed

Life becomes an adventure. Take this nondescript day in March 2022. Out and about on the bike – doing jobeens (Dada's term for small easily tick-offable errands). First up was the cobbler's. A pair of shoes I had left in without much expectation had been transformed. Clarks, sensible shoes but the type I thought couldn't have been soled: they were like new shoes. He had refurbished everything. Almost like Trigger's brush.

I love cobbler's shops. They are in some ways the last bastion of Shops That Don't Give a Shite About How They Look. There is no retail expert's report about maximizing footfall. This place *is* footfall manifested. There isn't a plant kept prisoner in the corner, a painting from an artist who held their nose while selling their worst corporate shite one. It's just a chest-high counter, nowhere to sit, shoes piled high, a general smell of Extreme Arts and Crafts glue off the place.

It looks chaotic, like a small AliExpress warehouse, but one person knows where everything is. And just like bicycles and tailors, this little shop fights climate change. Getting an extra year out of your shoes doesn't seem like much, but it means before you die you'll probably buy a few pairs less. Sorry to bring your death into it, and I hate that you have to hear it from me, but your life is finite, so if your shoes last longer you'll buy less. Don't wait until you've stopped giving a shit about what people think of you before serially getting shoes repaired. Do it now.

Before you do, a couple of tips.

- Nearly every shoe is fixable in some way. (Even runners. Perhaps not always by Old Mr Murphy the cobbler, but definitely by designey-type Young People with tattoos and short socks.)

- If you haven't been there in a while, it might be a bit dearer than you think. It won't be a fiver. Yes, you could technically get new shoes again instead, but they won't be broken in and have your foot curves on the insole. Believe me, *it's still worth it.*

- There's a strong chance the cobbler will be very pleased with how the job went. Take an extra minute to chat to them about how pleased they are. What a pleasure it will be to talk to someone who is happy in their job. (Even if they can't fix it, they can fix it – both of you will agree that it would be a shame to throw them out and you'd get another year out of them.) This is a pure mental health boost. Grab those boosts like vitamins where you can as we all grapple with the enormity of normal life as well as All This Climate Shit.

- Get to the tailor's as well. They will be up a narrow stairway buried under a pile of slacks.

The cobbler's was half ten in the morning. Then I went and got my phone fixed.

Whether it's marketing, lazy thinking or lazy acting, I always felt like phones weren't a fixy thing. Yes, the screen can be fixed. People are fixing screens in back streets and their own homes all over the place. I have waited in apartment car parks for that kind of thing. I assume they are all fully up to date with their tax affairs and will ask no further questions. But when the camera goes or the speaker goes, I just kind of assume it can't be fixed. There are no screws. If you bring it to the shop a 14-year-old sales assistant will just talk about it going back to the factory, but we both know that's like saying the dog's going to live on a farm. You can press the issue with them but they'll give you a look that says, *Why are you making this part-time job complicated? I'm at the start of my life and you are an Old Man. Let me make my own mistakes and choose my own path. Now, actually, I've looked you up on the System and you're entitled to an upgrade.* And generally I've taken the bait.

It's not phone-shop guy's fault. Phones are not meant to really be repaired. They are meant to last three years at the most. They are just part of built-in obsolescence – the greatest Lack of Confidence Trick in a whole line of psychological campaigns to turn consumers from the likes of my father – 'There's no lasting in anything nowadays' – into the likes of me – 'I was just *bored* with the old phone anyway.'

Typically it's the battery that wears you down by wearing itself down. Security Update Operating System version 13.1 downloads tear_the_hole_out_of_the_battery.exe. About 12 per cent of your waking time is spent thinking about cables, and you start seeing possible USB slots everywhere. Shouting on the train, 'WHY IS THIS CHARGING POINT NOT WORKING? THIS IS A THIRD WORLD COUNTRY,' and then the phone company appears like Clippy: *It looks like you have a phone with a shit battery. How ever could that have happened? Would you like an upgrade?*

I have my phone three years. I wake up every day and someone is offering me an upgrade. But the phone is FINE. It contains more memory than all the information ever recorded in the world from cave paintings until 2002. (And I've filled it up with pictures of my bald spot, but still. IT'S FINE.)

There comes a time in everyone's life when you realize that the point of printers is to sell ink, the point of social media is to sell your opinions without giving you a cut, and the point of a phone is to sell contracts, with most of the phones being sweeteners to welcome you in. *How much for this phone? A thousand euro. But if you sign a contract for four years I'll give you two phones and a Wispa.* It'll be the same with cars soon. At some point none of us will really *own* a car. We'll just drive one and buy updates. And actually fixing it without Elon Musk's blessing will be illegal.

So the tiniest act of just getting up off my hole and getting the camera on my phone fixed was literally the least I could do.

I brought it to that part of town where you bring phones and they fix them like it's a natural thing. In Dublin, this is in Moore Street.

Well! if I was in good form after the fixed shoes, the phone experience sent me over the top. I went into the shop full of 'I don't suppose you can' and 'I know it's a long shot' and the woman behind the counter countered with 'A new camera is €45, okay? How about €40? Say thirty minutes?' Carlsberg don't do phone-fixing situations, though I'm sure it's led to phone-breaking ones. Sure enough, when I came back she had it done and was just clearing up. She had a pile of phone hulks on the counter – a miniature breaker's yard on the pristine white shelf. She showed me the phone she'd taken the camera out of. I don't know why that seemed revolutionary to me.

Mending shoes and a phone. And it was only half eleven. It's enough to turn a grown man a bit odd. Next on the agenda was buying a sensible Christmas present for my mother in Marks & Spencer. I was queuing at the counter. Ahead of me was a woman returning what seemed like a hell of a lot of outfits.

'I work in the wardrobe department for a TV show,' she told the sales assistant by way of explanation for why she was bringing back twenty-five dresses. 'Do you have a bin – can I give you this suit bag?'

My ears pricked up. A perfectly good suit bag headed for the bin? This sounded like a job for Slightly Odd Man.

When she was gone, I asked the sales assistant if I could have the empty suit bag. I'd no idea what I was going to do with it. *But it'll come in handy for something.* That's the kind of person I am now. High-vis bicycle helmet, asking a puzzled sales assistant if he can take away a suit bag. The kind of person early-2000s-Dublin me would have looked at and said, 'You're making a show of yourself. Let her throw away the suit bag, for goodness' sake, the state of you. You didn't spend all them nights studying for exams to turn into a bit of a high-vis oddball.'

But I think that *is* me.

The whole system is a fix

The EU, for all its faults, has at least brought in some half-arse of an attempt to have the right to repair. Manufacturers in the EU will now be legally obliged to make sure some electronic goods such as tellies can be repaired for ten years. Makers can't be soldering components to motherboards or using screws that can only be opened with magic wands now. They have to facilitate third parties to fix things, supply manuals – you know, ordinary common decency.

There is still a shortage of spare parts, and the law itself still doesn't cover phones and laptops. Some tech companies have said they will voluntarily make manuals available, but everyone's waiting to see how that will turn out. Phone companies claim they don't want fly-by-nights repairing phones because . . . I don't know, it might open up a portal to the Underworld or reduce their profits – whichever is worse.

I understand why they're doing it. They don't want us to fix things because they want us to buy new ones. That's just how any company works. But e-waste and mining for new 'e' is awful for climate change, deforestation, ocean acidification. And the campaign for the right to repair has been going on a long time. It has made progress but there's a long way to go. The point is, even if you feel bad about how many electronics you're throwing away and how cheap everything is, it's deliberately hard for you to do the right thing. Don't feel bad. But find out.

It's such a pity fixing is made so hard. Fixing something is one of the most fulfilling things you can do. Admittedly, I'm easily pleased. Finding the start of the Sellotape for a child gives me a thrill. So you can imagine how much fun it is to change the blades on a Nutribullet successfully. And it brings you into the happy world of YouTube fixing videos, with slightly grouchy American oul' lads pottering around in their sheds. 'So what you wanna do here is you gotta get your screwdriver right here, right under . . . [grunt] and it shooooouuld pop out . . . [heavy breathing] and there you go.'

It looks like therapy for them, as if they're trying not to get angry with the skater-kids currently 'MAKING A GOSHDARNED RUCKUS OUTSIDE MY PROPERTY', but I follow them along and by the end of it, we're all happy. It makes a balls of the YouTube algorithm when you do venture down that route, though. The *Do you want to find the woman of your dreams?* ads start to replace the *Grammarly helps supercharge your CV* ones.

But either way, I ended up with the Nutribullet back in action. I was a proud man standing tall after that. In my newly dyed boots. Yes, flush from the success of completing a small maintenance task, I dyed a pair of boots that had printer ink splashed on them.

I have a grudging respect for how much a printer seems to dislike its owner. In a world where every iteration of technology wants to be intuitive, eager to please, a dog waiting for your next instruction, a printer doesn't give a damn. A printer is a cat, staring at you and smirking, asking to be fed but then ignoring the food. And one trick a printer has up its sleeve: ink will fall out if it's not level. Onto my boot.

When life hands you ink-stains, it's buy or dye. I did both boots. And they look nice.

I'm getting carried away. I haven't dyed anything since. I didn't launch a 450-issue Marshall Cavendish monthly magazine called *Domestic God: Knacky Stuff for the Beta Male*. (The first issue is 50 cent – I mean the price. I don't have any problems with the rapper – with a free bottle of dye, and each subsequent issue costs €11.) But I loved those boots. Even the cobbler liked the colour when I told him ALL about it.

We need to worship fixing as much as we frotter ourselves over innovation. I am *sick* of hearing about innovation. I want to hear about *maintenance*. Surely we've enough clothes, shoes and devices that there would be more cobbler's and tailor's and tech-repair shops than bookies and vape shops. Instead of dumping the WEEE in cages and not caring what city in the Global South it gets sent to to cause hazards, we should have e-junkyards on the edges of our own towns with motherboards scattered around the place and guarded by small dogs. I want today's children to experience the disappointment of a 1980s outing with your father that was purely about looking at scrap. I want working in computers to make people think of grimy-faced, laconic, tobacco-chewing mechanics, welding and soldering.

Maintenance people need to be heroes in our culture. If we can have a movie called *The Accountant* we can definitely have a bingeable Netflix series called *The Mechanic* – an upgrade from the standard maintenance-technician roles where the guy in overalls is the first to die. Innovators are always writing on glass walls, not wearing shoes and maybe eating an ice cream in the board-room to show their lack of respect for orthodoxy. Maintenance people wear hard-hats and grumble that it can't be done. Well, I want the movies re-shot with the maintenance guy telling the innovator, 'That'll be a nightmare to get at once the walls are plastered.'

I'm not talking about a load of steam-punk hipsters in coffee shops with Newcomen-engine-powered valve radios, winding the grandfather clocks on their wrists while playing chess with a mechanical Turk. Just a bit of respect for duct/duck tape, WD-40, glue, tiny screwdrivers, magnifying glasses you wear on your eye. Workshops. Small rooms above a shop, craftspeople. Innovation might drive the future but maintenance and mending keep the world ticking over. In a fractious world, let's get On The Mend.

Of course, some things are beyond fixing. You might need to get another one. And that's where there's more fun.

A second-hand up not handout

One of the things I find hardest to do on this journey of learning how wrong I am and starting to do some small right things – apart from doing the right thing – is not be judgemental. It's so much fun and cathartic. And *easy*. All you have to do is one small good thing, and then accuse anyone who doesn't join you of being PART OF THE PROBLEM. Make sure to ignore any other good things they might be doing or any legitimate questions they raise. It's the best fun.

The good and bad thing about getting older is you start getting too reasonable. Seeing other people's side of the story. I'm not talking about 'in fairness, he made a great job of the German economy'. I mean affability, reasonableness, but also a loss of necessary anger. I can go from 'WHAT ARE YOU DOING TO THAT LOVELY WHITETHORN HEDGE, YOU MONSTER?' to 'Oh, maybe they're creating lateral branch structures and not letting individual trees dominate. They're actually creating a better foundation for a habitat.' I try not to condemn anyone too much in this book. I wanted an entire chapter called 'Arseholes' just to give out about arseholes but, you know, maybe they're not so bad. I also wanted to rant about unboxing. But I'm not going to do it.

Unboxing is the huge online entertainment phenomenon where kids and adults watch videos of other humans taking toys and gadgets out of their packaging. Huge emphasis is placed on the actual experience of opening the packaging. I could make snarky points about how the simple joy of opening a present has been co-opted into a giant industrial marketing machine that made money for YouTube, toy manufacturers and a few thousand influencers, changed the packaging industry and then deceived children into believing that what was in fact a very sophisticated advertisement was just another child opening a toy. How it encouraged consumerism, excessive packaging, made a virtue of built-in obsolescence. But I won't include that. I was also about to start shouting that you CAN'T JUST ADD 'UN' TO ANYTHING TO MAKE A NEW WORD and that we need to unstart that trend. But I won't do that either. Language is fluid, and other people's pedantry is annoying, and the word unboxing is the least of our problems. (But trust me, if we ever get out the other side of this there will be a huge clampdown on words and phrases that annoy me. Today I'm mostly fuming about *living their best life*.)

I just try to understand and again say, Not Instead But As Well.

I completely understand why it's attractive. Unwrapping something. Watching other people unbox and their excitement. There is a human connection there. You are experiencing their joy. The beautiful lines of the box in question, the ASMR appeal of the sound of hasps being undone or the crinkle of the paper. If you can forget that they are 11 and making eight million dollars a year.

My wife's family have a tradition of packing some presents in old Cornflakes boxes to sort of obscure the shape of the gift inside. 'Coco Pops – just what I've always wanted!' the recipient jokes. Then they take out the rolled-up newspaper and eventually find the voucher. (It's great for taking the vouchery look off voucher presents.) Uncornflakesboxing is lovely. So why shouldn't the glossier version be too? I'm not going to say whether unboxing is just another depressing symptom of our consumerist culture or . . . whatever the other option was.

So far my children have not been exposed to unboxing. But it is only a matter of time. As they get older I can feel the Toy World crowding in on them. It was easier before. You could get them something educational and made of wood. But the serpent appeared to them in the garden and said, 'Why are you not playing with plastic shite with unrealistic body shapes?' And their eyes were opened and they felt shame. So now they have Barbies.

Like most things on this 'journey', our Christmas presents are a mixed bag.

My wife and I exchange some new things. Like books. But books are exempt from all discussions of sustainability. I'm sorry, I won't tolerate any debate on that. Let me repeat. New Books Are Not the Problem. You should not feel in any way guilty about buying new books and then recommending to friends that they get their own copy, possibly two. I'm sorry, I don't make the rules.

I recently bought my wife an electric screwdriver because she is getting into DIY, and nothing says 'I love you and understand you and the passing years have done nothing to diminish the spark in our marriage' like an electric screwdriver. I bought her trees a few times. They'll be planted in a scheme in the countryside somewhere. I assume they will. The whole thing could be a Ponzi (or Pine-zi) scheme for all I know. But if someone's gonna take me for a ride, I want it to be for planting a tree rather than DDT.

My wife bought me the first nice razor I've owned since the Y2K bug. A luxury open-comb object without a smidge of plastic, as metal as Rammstein. The box says that that two billion disposable razors are thrown away every year. Not by me, they're not. I think I have the same rotating cast of disposable razors for the last decade. Some come in and out of favour. They're like band members of the Fall who keep rubbing Mark E. Smith (my chin) up the wrong way. But there's a new lead zinger in town now, and the others can act as back-up.

The children get at least some new toys. It's unavoidable. *Bluey* – the Australian cartoon about a dog – has some toys that go with it. Of course. Although I won't hear a word said against *Bluey*. Any cartoon that sneaks in a conversation between two dad dogs about vasectomies seems all right to me. So I'll tolerate a bit of plastic for *Bluey*. If they had fun playing with the new toys, I had even more fun finding the second-hand ones. If you have the time and the internet access, a reasonable tolerance for dealing with strangers and the nosiness that particularly comes with having small children and generally taking an interest in other people's lives, I cannot recommend highly enough the experience of buying and selling second-hand stuff online.

Let's start with toys, a great place to start. Very few toys can be recycled because they're often made of loads of equally cheap, hard-to-recover shite. So they go to landfill or, in certain cases, the garden of that house that's been Sale Agreed for four years.

I read a survey (let's not trouble ourselves where – you didn't get this book in the science section) that found a quarter of parents surveyed admitted to throwing away toys that were unused and on average children had four unplayed-with toys. Aside from the waste, consider the absolute tragedy of an unplayed-with toy. Why would you do that to them? Have you not seen *Toy Story*? It's heartbreaking. Unplayed-with toys? Possibly the worst feature of the military-industrial complex.

Why not give those toys a new life? And have a good old nose around the house of whoever you're buying them from? It's the next level of the computer game that is Raising Children. It starts before you have children. You assemble the war chest – the array of equipment and clothing, the various hoppers and skippers and jumpers, the giant bags of eight hundred babygros, marvelling at the size of them. The little *shoes*. LOOK AT THE LITTLE SHOESIES.

Toy-buying is a preview of the chaos of toddler-rearing. The door is answered by a wordless toddler, staring curiously like an uncontacted tribesperson, chewed cream cracker in their hand along with Mammy's car keys and the gas bill. Their exhausted parents come to the door, hand over the toy, take my cash and use it to pay for pizza and gin.

I go home and look their house up on the house price website to see how much it sold for.

Sometimes the exchange is in a neutral location. Two dads meeting in a Lidl car park in a midlands town early on a Sunday morning. A car pulls in. I've even passed the goods over without getting out of the car – a fella drove in so we were driver door to driver door like the FBI do it. 'Are you Colm from Adverts?' he said. 'I am,' I said. 'Did you bring it?' We look around to make sure the other hasn't been tailed.

Then he hands over the breast pump. I bought dollies from a man in a railway station. He had to quit work due to an accident but now makes a few bob roaming all over the country with his free travel buying and selling things. A modern-day pedlar.

On the other side, I am endlessly overjoyed by the stuff that people will take from me. When we're doing a clear out, we're about take it to the tip, I think, *Maybe I'll just see who wants it online.* If you believe that there is a lid for every pot, a foot for every shoe, a soul for every mate, then, my friend, you will have a happy time Getting Rid of Free Shit online.

I put things up in trepidation. Sometimes there's a clamour; sometimes there's tumbleweed (complete indifference from other hoarders, I haven't seen anyone give away tumbleweed yet). But eventually nearly everything finds a new home. 'A broken watch, a box of stuff and a battered chair, old attic flooring, a bit of carpet, a load of leads (I don't know what they're for), 11 feet of electrical cable or four Penneys blankets, one with a stain.'

And it's not just the stuff. It's the stories. A garden table to replace one that was stolen that morning by someone hopping over the wall while the owner was in the shower. A box of six hundred event wristbands (don't ask) that will be used for a charity bath-tub race. I shovelled a pile of dirt to fill a hole into the back of a van for a grateful buyer. (To be fair, I had advertised it as 'a pile of dirt that may be useful to fill a hole'.) A woman drove through a snowstorm to get a damaged cooker splashback. Each time, people have walked away from our door clutching things like they were the final missing part in their Big Plan.

Sometimes a puzzled spouse is sent to collect it. They walk away carrying ten fitted-kitchen plinth feet wondering if maybe this is getting out of hand.

And if the human interaction isn't rich enough, there is always the glorious intrigue of the online review section. You can review the person who you bought or sold from. A positive or a negative. I focus on the negative ones to see what went wrong. I tell myself this is so I can avoid the pitfalls of poor communication or disappointment. Because I have a 100 per cent positive record. I might drive a diesel but I knows how to . . . er . . . pleasel. Also because I am a ghoul feasting on the prana of humans' emotional energy. It is intriguing to see how people who have successfully and positively dealt with strangers hundreds of times drop the ball so severely that their one negative review is 'DO NOT LISTEN TO THIS MAN. HE IS A LIAR'. What went wrong? How did the relationship break down so much?

Either way, this is a hell of a lot more interesting than going to H&M and hating myself in the changing-room mirror.

Fierce value altogether

You could always get cheap clothes, but somewhere along the line they got even cheaper, and people started throwing them out because there just weren't enough people to buy them from the charity shops, and somehow our clothes are ending up in dumps in other countries.

I have cheated the fast-fashion industry. I buy at fast-fashion prices but wear them for slow-clothing-movement durations.

But I don't think we should be shaming people who buy fast fashion. You don't need to spend more than ten minutes with your head in the world to know that a man who knows sweet FA about clothing, who is in the comfortable years of not having to forge an identity or keep up with a peer group, is completely the wrong person to be lecturing anyone about whether they got enough wears out of their Boohoo top. Just like with flying, pure shaming isn't always effective. Whenever I feel shamed for my awfulness to the planet, my first reaction is *Well, fuck you so, I'll do more of the bad thing, ya bollox. How do you like that?* That reaction is followed by crippling shame and continuing to do the bad thing while ashamed. A Catholic upbringing serves me well in that respect. But when someone takes the time to patiently and non-judgementally explain how the bad thing is bad but where I could start to do less bad thing, takes the time to tell me the impact of my actions, gives me a bit of space to think, then they'll get a much better outcome. Or at least that's what I tell them, hoping they'll go away.

So if you don't have a whole lot of money and you'd like to buy something that looks expensive and fashionable and it's right there in the shop in front of you, it's going to be hard to find the starting point. But do get curious – about the impact of fast fashion on the environment and the people who make it, about the alternatives, the second-hand, the smaller producers. Is it a fashion item or is it a particular style you're looking for? Hang on . . . I am seriously out of my depth here. What I mean is . . . *Look, what's wrong with the jumper you have? Isn't it grand and warm? When I was a child all I had was one good jumper, one second-best jumper and the one for painting. And there's you with your jumper hardly worn at all and me out there every day working my fingers to the bone and the INGRATITUDE* . . . Sorry, the mask is slipping. What I actually mean is that one good place to start is knowing the positive impact of simply getting a few more wears out of something. According to UK studies, if you got an extra nine months out of an item of clothing you could reduce the carbon footprint by a sixth. Now nine months is a long time to be staring at the same top, especially if you had a shit night out in it at the start of those nine months, but if you're looking for a simple place to start, try and find out the carbon cost per wear. It's a small, achievable target where the cost comes down immediately if you wear something *one* more time . . . and then two and then three. (It's like when you bought that monthly cinema pass that one time and the cost per cinema trip halved immediately after you went to the second film in a month.) Before long you're like me, wearing the same clothes so often, they're practically sequestering the carbon.

And if you're worried that eventually buying less will put garment workers in developing countries – and also the UK – out of a job because 'any job is better than no job', then your guilt would be better off spent researching the impact of boycotts. It's not as clear as you think. Finding out what the workers themselves actually want is a better use of your time. It's a classic thing we do in the consumer countries – we buy a load of stuff from a lower-income country, find out it's a bad thing, then feel guilty and drop them like a hot snot *without ever considering their agency or what they want.* That goes for a lot of things we think about when trying to do something about this Giant Thing.

- Do the bad thing.

- Find out about the bad thing.

- Stop doing the bad thing in a panic.

- Rush into some other thing because the label says 'Not as bad as the other thing'.

- Which turns out to be a different bad thing (biofuels, avocados, organic cotton tote bags for life).

- Find out and feel bad and then say, 'AH, WHAT'S THE POINT!'

So when it comes to fast fashion, I would say read up first before flagellating yourself about your three hundred black tops from Penneys. Or flagellate yourself with one of your Penneys tops. It's technically getting an extra wear out of it anyway.

A top in the ocean

I was getting a bit excited thinking about having stuff mended, getting stuff second-hand, about adventures in car parks and standing in apartment lobbies with malfunc-tioning lights waiting with my €10 for Madame Gazelle's Schoolroom, like I was getting somewhere. Then I saw an article about there being so many unsold fast-fashion clothes dumped in the Atacama desert in Chile that it was visible from space and I thought, *What's the fucking point? It's just a drop in the ocean. Or rather, or on land.*

Look, I know. You feel powerless. The *only* thing to do is take a slightly longer view. That things are shit but they change. That pile of clothes in the Atacama, okay, that exists now. It doesn't prevent me from carrying on trying. All steps are tiny. My wife has started buying stuff on Depop, the big second-hand clothing site. I bought second-hand earphones this year online for the first time in my life on Back Market. Neither of us knew these places existed a year ago. They don't exist because of people like me with my forty-something inertia. They exist because of Generation Z and Alpha and whatever they're calling young people now. These small decisions are not going to save diddlysquat on the planet, but they represent how quickly things change. Trust. Trusting that second-hand online buying is reliable.

The main power we have is that Companies That Sell Nice Fun Stuff don't have our money yet. Or not all of it. And they want you buying their stuff for the rest of your life. So if you start acting like the planet is important to you and asking FastFashionFuckYeahGiveMeMoney, a clothing company I just made up, what their circular economy plan is, and another few million people (all readers of this book) do the same, they start to listen. They already know everything about us – social media tracks thousands of pieces of data on us. (That's why they knew you wanted those Daisy Dukes, Declan.) So let them know you care.

According to a report from the Economist Intelligence Unit, half of the leaders of the clothing industry believe consumers are driving the increased focus on sustainability issues in the fashion and textile industry. Now I'm sure the other half aren't hearing consumers saying, 'G'wan away, fuckit, tis grand.'

I reckon they're just not hearing much from them at all. So say something. Especially you, older people. People who think they've done their sustaining in the eighties. We're not done. We haven't even begun.

5.

It's in me nature

*'Name one difference between a tree
and a flower? A tree is much larger.'*

'What is wind? Wind is air in a hurry.'

**– Excerpts from Colm O'Regan's third-class Nature
copy, Tuesday, 16 September 1986**

'I'm never bothered by trees'

**– Dada when asked whether the small tree near
him in the restaurant was in his way**

Friday and Saturday nights, the door of the sitting room
would be flung open. Dada would look at the fire that we
hadn't been minding properly. They were coming down.
The migration of Mama and Dada from the kitchen – where
the Wellstood cooker or range had been turned off to save

on th'oil – to the sitting room, where the open fire burned in the grate. The oil shock wasn't just about the fuel in the car. An unnecessarily burning range felt like leaking money up the chimney. And heat did leak out of every part of the house. There was never a danger of radon gas building up in an old farmhouse.

Dada brought the telly with them. Or one of the brothers did. It was a rite of passage for each of the boys to become strong enough to lift the telly down to the parlus, as he called it. Dada didn't speak Irish but Irish words littered his speech. The telly was the size of a heist-movie safe and weighed as much. It was mounted on the sideboard and plugged in, and on Friday nights we'd watch *Dallas*. A TV show where no one was switching off the oil. Unless it was a ruse to trick Cliff Barnes out of his share. We'd sip our weekend treat, Tanora, as we watched Sue Ellen fix herself a stiff drink from the decanter. Imagine! They had enough room in the house to have a special table, with no newspapers on it, just for putting the drink on. Then we'd all look away or cough when there was a sex scene and hope they cut swiftly to the post-coital L-shaped bed sheets that showed the belly button of the man and the chin of the woman. On Saturday the door was flung open – okay, that's an exaggeration; Dada was not a flinger – and the *Late Late Show* was brought down, and we'd watch the standard eighties line-up: a combination of Peter Ustinov, a post-punk band bemusing the studio audience and hopefully an awkward interview, punctuated by long silences, with a drunk actor or a smoking Tom Waits. Then in 1986 the two shows switched places, causing a seismic shift in the country.

Whether it was Friday or Saturday, the arrival of the telly was preceded by Dada livening up the fire and making it ready for A Big Block. 'Do you see that?' Dada would say as he propped the Probably Too Big Block into the fireplace with a poker. 'That's elm now.' And say no more. Elm. The byword for BTU-dense heat. A rock you could burn. Giving one last burst of life after a cruel fate.

Dada was fierce cut up over the elms. Depending on your age, you might only know about Dutch elm disease via clips from the RTÉ archives from the early eighties. A clip of a beautiful tree trunk on the ground next to a brown Ford Cortina and a tree surgeon's lorry no bigger than your average modern family SUV all set up to take it away. The elms that got the plague the worst were the English elms that came to Ireland from Europe in the 1700s. They were planted in hedges enclosing the land as part of 'an exciting new project set to bring Irish agriculture to newer heights', as it was described in a post on Ye-LinkedIn at the time. Then the fungus came and, because they were genetically not very diverse, it wiped them out. Elms were the lumper potatoes of trees. I have vague memories of the disease emptying out the grove, a small triangle of trees near the house that appeared to a four-year-old to be a massive forest. But I remember more clearly the timber, and Dada mourning the loss of the grand trees that he loved when he first moved to Dripsey and how the Dutch elm destroyed the ditches he fell in love with.

So like a lot of farmers, he set about replacing them – in his case with fast-growing poplars. He knew himself they were only oul' soft shite, but he just wanted to take the bare look off the grove and other ditches around the place.

And they're still there – 30, 40 feet tall. Nothing as majestic as his favourite tree on the farm, a horse chestnut in the Inch, but they were a balm for him. And Dada planted other trees around the area and would point them out to me. 'I planted that blue cedar there,' he'd say. They're his little mementoes around the place.

Not everyone likes trees. It is a weird quirk of Ireland that we spend half our time giving out about The Brits and How They Stole Our Trees For Their Armada, but to look at us officially we seem to hate them. For every chain-wearing official with a sparkling clean shovel turning the sod on a little sapling for a tree-planting ceremony for an important new development, there is someone going mad with a saw bringing down a hundred-year giant CO_2 lung of a tree. Sometimes this is part of clear-felling in coniferous woods: other times it's on spurious health and safety grounds, ordered by authorities paranoid about being sued. Local groups complain about trees being used for anti-social behaviour as if anti-social behavers are rebels hiding out in forests launching their unspecified attacks from behind a 6 foot apple tree. Sometimes it's developers who know they can cram a few more tear-sodden apartments into the foot-print of one oak. And sometimes it's just people with saws who think saws will go stale if they're not used on trees. Also, there are curious overreactions.

'Excuse me, could we just make that woodland walk a bit more accessible for those with extra needs?'

'What's that? Bulldoze a ten-yard-wide strip, killing all the nature you came to see?'

'No . . . no, just a bit of trim, just a few briars and enough for someone using a wheelchair.'

'SORRY, I CAN'T HEAR YOU OVER THIS BULLDOZER – YOU'LL HAVE TO CALL THE OFFICE.'

I'm sure that's a gross simplification but we do need to mind our big trees. There's a lot of fuss about planting trees, but there are 700 million trees in the country already, and the good ones are quietly snorting up two stone of CO_2 every year. Minding their own business. Maybe we should be valuing them too instead of patting ourselves on the back for planting new trees. But of course you don't get as much kudos for leaving a tree there as for planting a new one.

Getting kudos for planting new trees

I snuck out of home at dawn. When I say *snuck*, I wasn't defying my parents. I just didn't want to wake the children. And when I say dawn, it was winter so the dawn is not a stretch. I was carrying four trees, a shovel, a spade and a fork and walking about half a mile to plant the trees. I felt self-conscious and stupid. It's one thing to get up on stage and tell stories about how you're an eejit. That's an act. You have a role to play. People understand why your head is above that particular parapet. Despite what you might think, and that it might be your worst nightmare, it's safe as houses. You get to snark and have an opinion and not be fact-checked and, the odd heckler aside, you're not really challenged that much. Except by the vast gaping emptiness that greets a joke that doesn't land. Or some fucker on their phone up the front Insta

Live-ing their experience to their four followers. (Those two incidents may be related.) But it's a manageable level of discomfort for me. It's actually harder to be earnest, out and about with a spade, a bit of a busybody-looking fella. The committEE-man. Carrying tools into the public space. You look odd. Well, I thought I did anyway. *Where's he going?* I assumed the people on the Luas were wondering. The tools kept falling off my sloping shoulders and getting tangled in the tree branches. I hoped no one noticed.

I got up onto a patch of spare ground near a very busy junction. I put down the stuff and tried to look at home. People watched me as they passed. I felt naked. I'd forgotten my magic high-vis, the force field that makes an oddball look more official. *I don't know what he's doing but he's supposed to be there anyway because he was wearing the high-vis.*

But from the first moment I sank the spade into the ground, and marked out the foot or so square, I knew I was in the right place. I know it sounds like something you'd see on Facebook with a sunset in the background and Lucida Handwriting font, but planting a tree that doesn't directly benefit you feels really good. Especially an apple tree. I imagined children of all races playing some sort of simple running game or perhaps with a stick. It was a hot day in my daydream. (Seasonably so. We'd fixed the climate thing.) And the children would quench their thirst with the apples of the tree I'd planted. I'd be floating in the clouds somewhere watching them, but not in a weird way. A Gody way. The story of Johnny Appleseed is buried somewhere in my brain. Possibly from the Rainbow series of English readers we had in primary school in the 1980s – a lighter-hearted alternative to the stories of Minotaur-eating youths. From my memory,

Johnny Appleseed was a genial old man who went around dropping seeds out of a bag all over North America, planting thousands of orchards for the benefit of generations to come, all out of the goodness of his heart, with birds landing on his fingers amid noble pow-wows with Native American chiefs who respected him because it obviously never occurred to them to plant anything. With some trepidation, I googled him recently, on the lookout for *Why Planting Apple Trees Is Problematic* articles. It turns out John Chapman was very real but he wasn't some misty-eyed idealist letting seeds fall out of the hole at the bottom of a burlap sack. He was – to use vernacular Irish people would be well familiar with – a pure cute hoor. This was at start of the nineteenth century, when an entire continent was being opened up – excuse me, stolen – for use by settlers. Private companies were buying up land in advance of the huddled masses moving west. A company called the Ohio Company of Associates had a deal: whoever was up for going out beyond the pale and setting up a home would get a hundred acres of land. To prove they were serious, settlers had to plant seventy trees – fifty apple, twenty peach. So Johnny Appleseed gently meandered very purposefully ahead of the envelope of settlement, planting orchards, selling them to settlers and then moving on, like Wallace and Gromit laying tracks ahead of the train. And the apple trees were all for cider, so there weren't going to be any flaxen-haired children picking them to quench their thirst. They would be for whatever the nineteenth century's equivalent was of silage-men drinking pint bottles of Bulmers with ice. (But back then flaxen-haired children were into the cider too. In fact, many people in the American West were permanently a bit hammered, as cider was *just a thing you drank*.)

I digress to this because often what looks like Pure Altruism is also people Up To Something. Not that it's a bad thing, but you should be careful about telling the world you're just doing a good thing and be open about any other reasons you have for doing it.

But I swear, these apple trees were not for a land grab. I wasn't going to plant an orchard and then sell the land for a hotel to be built on. We are just a group of locals planting a few trees in spare corners around the place. I won't speak for others in the tree-planting group, but I am definitely doing this to alleviate a sense of powerlessness. It's also a stepping stone to being the type of person who does that kind of thing (see 'That Wouldn't Be for Me at All', page 156).

So I know it's a little naïve and these little trees might only absorb, relatively speaking, the square root of fuck-all carbon in their lifetime before some langer kicks them over. (About half the trees we planted have been kicked over or stolen – hopefully by someone who knows what to do with a tree). But that kind of disappointment is merely the building up of one's setback muscles for what's to come.

Then we started delivering trees to private houses. I planted one or two, flush with Johnny Appleseed confidence, for people in the area. Just like my father did. And this is not virtue signalling, but I swear to god I was high after planting the tree. Like, pure intrinsic high. Not even a high based on people thinking what a great boy I was altogether. (I am, though – say I am, will you?) Just me walking away feeling good about myself, knowing no one knew it was me apart from those who have to go to work at eight on a Sunday morning. And obviously telling you all about it in this book.

Rehabilitating nature, replacing lost biodiversity, changing the way we look at trees . . . that's a tall order and won't be achieved in the short term by some fella in a high-vis planting a few apple trees in a spare corner. And ultimately, we fix biodiversity with large-scale nature recovery, thousands of square miles at a time; we fix climate change by not digging stuff up from the ground and burning it to let the carbon out. But our few trees have their little benefit nearby, and, sorry for the wankiness, planting did change me just a smidge, made me bolder.

It wasn't as glamorous in year two at the start. Mainly we were replacing the trees lost to attrition. Some of the attrition was because I'd planted them in a place that . . . well, let's just say if you were drinking cans in the dark, you might have bumped into them. And others were stolen by the subset of thieves who are also tree enthusiasts. But the confidence and the networks and the knowhow came together just before season's end, when 250 whips (very small saplings) were going abegging from Coillte, and we came together and planted them in a few hours in the corners of a park. Legally this time. The 'difficult second album' of doing something like this is nearly more important. Because you have to stick at it. You're not just doing something for the planet or your own mental health or to act the Big Tree-Planting Man or for the community: you're also representing the concept of doing something. And if you just piss off after one year, you're telling other people, *Ah yeah, that's just a bit of fly-by-night effort.* (As it turns out a lot of year 2's trees have also fecked off but so what? Year 3 is only a few weeks away.)

Just act natural

It doesn't come naturally to me to do this. For someone who has somehow made a book about a planet-wide crisis ALL ABOUT HIMSELF, it's still an effort to drag myself out there. And I don't have a feel for it. I'm not really that nature-y. I may have grown up on a farm, but that doesn't mean I was frolicking in the furze singing songs to the birds of the air while they alighted on my outstretched arm. Hedgehogs and voles didn't suspend hostilities to gather at my feet. I was bookish as a preteen and then obsessed with my martyrdom on the altar of ALL THE STUPID PEOPLE as a teenager.

I will say I did lots of picturesque smoking. If you live in the country and want to smoke various things without your parents knowing, you end up in some idyllic places. There can be a lot of staring at trees enigmatically. And of course there was that one summer I was a human scarecrow, but other than that ... **RECORD SCRATCH** '*What?*'

Okay, brief digression. One year a man who grew vegetables rented our fields. And as part of the deal he agreed to take me on – to be one of his army who picked the broccoli and cauliflower in the fields. A sacred job where boys and girls went at the start of the summer pale and spongey and came back battle-hardened and lean. Their hands were callused, fingernails framed with honest dirt, combat trousers and boots crusted with soil. And I would soon be one of them.

Unfortunately, it was not to be. The first morning I cycled over to the yard, the owner hurtled up to me in the jeep and roared out the window, *'Cmon away, I've a job for you.'*

We drove for ten minutes in silence before he abruptly turned off the public road and shuddered the jeep down a rutted and stony country lane. The lane eventually widened out into the headland of a field of what looked to be young cauliflower.

A flock of pigeons flew up at the approach of the jeep.

'Look at them hoors eating the young plants.'

'Bastards they are,' I said.

He paused and looked at me. 'Bastards is right,' he agreed. We seemed to have bonded.

We got out and stood looking at the fields. The pigeons landed again 20 yards away. One appeared to give us the finger.

'They'll ruin this crop. Five fields of cauliflower and they'll eat every fucking plant. They take no notice of the banger – they're too cute for that.'

Just then the gas banger went off. I jumped. A nearby pigeon raised an eyebrow and continued eating profits.

'See all those fields, right? What you'll do now is keep walking through these fields all day waving your arms at the pigeons to move them on. Never let the fuckers settle. Do that for a week and we'll see how they like that.'

I stared at him. The question *So you want me to be a human scarecrow?* was frozen on my lips. I looked around for a hidden-camera-show production team.

Without a further word, he got into the jeep and sped off. No one was left except me and the pigeons. That age-old enemy. Wits and brains and guile versus me.

The first day at work as a human scarecrow passed slowly. As did the following six weeks. Each day I arrived I vaguely expected some sort of reveal, but there was nothing. Maybe this *was* my job, although that proved to be a difficult sell to the lads in Dripsey, who would run around waving their arms shouting 'Caw caw' when I arrived. *Bastards*, I thought, preferring the company of pigeons at this stage.

Gradually I accumulated some creature comforts to make the days easier. I made a little shelter under a whitethorn tree. My father brought over the passenger seat of one of the scrapped Fiat Mirafioris. But even though I was outdoors, I was not foraging and hunting, observing the birds to see which berries were edible, learning the names of plants. I was not Bear Grylls using my own piss as shaving foam. Once I'd cycled around the headlands of the fields scaring the pigeons away, I went back to my hide, reading every book in the house from *The Butcher Boy* to *A Matter of Medicine* – an early Mills & Boon about a lantern-jawed doctor married to his work and a doe-eyed nurse who taught him how to love again. But it worked. The crop was saved.

Now, I'm not saying we should send our youth out into the fields to fight pests to cure their attention spans and sedentary lifestyles in one fell swoop instead of using glyphosate and bangers. Not yet, anyway. We'll wait for the wolves to be reintroduced and then they can sound the alarm.

But despite being 'quite rural', I never saw nature as all-encompassing. An infinitely complex system. It was a thing we dealt with. For some a hobby, for others a rival. A school subject, a thing separate to all of us. External. A thing that gets tamed and broken by humans and then sometimes gets fixed.

And I was raised on easy fixes.

The other Lord of the Rings

Our world is in peril. Gaia, the spirit of the Earth, can no longer stand the terrible destruction plaguing our planet. She sends five magic rings to five special young people: Kwame, from Africa, with the power of Earth; from North America, Wheeler, with the power of Fire; from Eastern Europe, Linka, with the power of Wind; from Asia, Gi, with the power of Water; and from South America, Ma-Ti, with the power of Heart. When the five powers combine, they summon Earth's greatest champion, Captain Planet. The power is yours!

Remember that? I lapped that stuff up. It was great for 'raising awareness'. Each episode of Captain Planet dealt with discrete, fixable problems caused by particular eco-villains who each had different specialities. Hoggish Greedly – overconsumption; Verminous Skumm – urban blight, disease and, er, drug dealing; Duke Nukem – nuclear power, usually to be found dumping sludge in a forest stream. There were poachers and an episode about AIDS. They even dipped their toes into the dodgy waters of over-population. Not to mention a trip to Northern Ireland, in 1992, in an episode called 'If It's Doomsday, This Must Be Belfast', with Catholics who say things like 'Saints alive'.

Captain Planet was also famous because everyone who was anyone got to play a villain. Jeff Goldblum, Meg Ryan, Sting, Martin Sheen, Tim Curry, Malcolm McDowell – at some point they all got to say, 'You'll pay for this, Captain Planet!' Whoopi Goldberg was Gaia for a while.

At the end of every episode the bad thing was fixed. The forest restored. And although it was a cartoon, it sort of seeped in that there were just bad guys who did bad things for bad-guy reasons. Duke Nukem seemed to just love radioactive sludge. He took baths in the stuff. It wasn't clear why. Just normal Bad Guy shit I suppose.

Things like this and *FernGully: The Last Rainforest* seeped into me, the idea that you can 'fix' the environment with quick fixes. And I'm sure I'm not the only one. A problem occurs. We need to do something. This is something. Do it.

And psychologically, it's a pain in the hole. If that's anatomically possible. It's one thing to get bad news; it's even more depressing to find out the thing to fix the bad news does harm to nature as well.

> 'All the trees are being cut down: quick, plant new
> ones. They take in carbon and they look natural.'

'What kind of trees?'

'Fast ones, I suppose. We haven't time to be investigating. Do you want to fix this thing or not? Stop doing reports!'

[Sometime later] 'Okay, they were the wrong trees. I'll never plant another tree again.'

Or the bees.

'Quick, the bees are in trouble.'

'Which bees?'

'I don't know – like, bees. How many bees are there?'

'Well, in Ireland, there are domesticated bees and then more than nine –'

'JUST GET LOADS OF BEES!'

[Sometime later] 'Okay, it turns out the domesticated bees are out-competing the wild bees and may, in fact, be contributing to the decline of the other ninety-nine species of bee no one told me about.'

'Ninety-nine species of bee – where? I only see one. Yerra, fuck the bees so.'

I find myself getting cross with animals for being 'difficult' about things. Can't they see we're trying to help? We had a wormery. It's a box, about the size of a microwave that you'd find dumped in a ditch. There's a long list of things that you can't give them. When I first read it, I was thinking, *Onions? Finicky feckers, aren't they, these worms? They'll eat it and they'll be glad of it. I was two minutes in the door with them and already I was their mother.*

The same with the poor bees. There are concerns that bee-bricks and bee-hotels could do more harm than good if they're not designed properly or cleaned, as they could lead to the spread of mites. OH, WELL, EXCUSE ME FOR TRYING TO HELP, BEES. I GIVE UP.

As you can imagine, this is not a helpful attitude. By taking it personally, I am wasting time.

I read a statistic that said something like 100 per cent of everything is fucked or nearly fucked. We don't really have time for my frustration. There comes a time, wrote the eminent psychiatrist Carl Jung, where you need to get the fuck over yourself.

So here's what I do when it comes to despair and futility, when it feels like nature is collapsing all around me.

Two rights don't even make a right

However complex you think it is, it's more complex and you're wrong but gradually getting less wrong, so don't take it personally.

First things first. It was probably obvious to others, but plebs like me are gradually appreciating that climate, air, water, soil and biodiversity are all part of the same giant system. Every little thing impacts in some way on the things next to it and sometimes the things farther away.

I used to think that climate change is happening because we're doing one bad thing – burning stuff. And biodiversity loss is happening because we're doing another bad thing – killing things and turning things' homes into car parks and land for growing things we eat – and the two are separate. Turns out we are so adept at generating positive-feedback-looping clusterfucks that we can't even predict how bad it will get. So when we try to fix one thing we break another. Like trampling over a moorhen's nest just to pick up some litter (I nearly did this, by the way).

On a larger scale, if you build a wind farm to burn less oil to make electricity, that's a good thing, right? But if you're going to build it in the middle of a bog and destabilise a mountainside so that in heavy rain brackish peaty water is washed into rivers, reducing the oxygen in the water and killing fish and disrupting the gravel breeding grounds, then you have to ask yourself, is that the right place to build a wind farm and is that a good enough thing?

Or take krill. I know you do. Probably in a supplement, actually. Could ye not leave one thing alone, for f–. Sorry, I promised myself I wouldn't krill-shame. Krill is a type of small shrimp that exists in its billions in the southern ocean. Krill oil is used as a supplement to lower cholesterol. It's also food for whales, but while it's hanging around, it actually affects climate change. It eats CO_2-eating algae and shites pellets of pure carbon that sink to the sea floor and stay there. So while you're objecting to your local cycle lane, this little dude is trying to keep the planet from turning into Venus.

The easiest example of this to understand is the bogs in Ireland. I thought for years we were ripping up a *habitat* to burn for heat, energy and employment. That that was the trade-off. But it turns out the peat was storing a load of CO_2 deep down in its pores. So when we cut it – I mean, it wasn't me but I've definitely burned briquettes so I helped – that CO_2 went into the atmosphere. Now Ireland's biggest ever carbon sink is being restored bit by bit.

This stuff used to be easier in the *Captain Planet* days. Coal mine in a forest? Bad. Wind farm? Reclaim bog for farm-land? What could be wrong with that? Good.

If you plant a load of the same species of tree to suck in carbon, meaning it's a monoculture, which means disease spreads more quickly and you'll have to cut the forest down and you can't even use it for furniture, then it's a bad thing. If you want a wildflower garden you can't just buy 'wILdD-FloWer sEeDs' from PoundLand. They're probably dressed with cyanide and full of rhododendrons. You have to find out what is suitable for your area because nature is different in different places. Rewilding is grand if every animal in the eco system is around, but rewilding with deer and no wolves means the trees won't grow. Nature would wreck your head. Which seems fair revenge.

If you drain the absolute shite out of a flood plain to alleviate flooding and then the city at the mouth of the river floods because water just 'gets everywhere', then that's a bad thing. We need floodable land. It's there for a reason. We spend so much time tidying nature's messy house, but nature is like my parents' house. They had a system. They knew where that appointment letter from the doctor was before

I decided to 'make it easier for them' and rearrange things in a way that only made sense to me.

These are all things we thought were a good idea because we were just focusing on fixing one problem, not thinking about the whole network.

Me too. Some of the trees I planted were planted in the wrong place and had to be moved. I was wrong. I took it personally. 'Can't they see I'm trying to save the planet?' I muttered through gritted teeth. But this isn't about me. So I got up early one morning and me and a few others moved the trees. And I got on with my life. Our anxiety about other trees being cut is not a reason to make up for it by throwing trees at the problem. Good working relationships with everyone will get more done in the end. Even if it feels slower at the time.

One other vital part of any natural system is the humans. We have an *awful* habit of trying to fix nature while forgetting to ask the people already living in the nature. Or assuming that all the people affected by a change are exactly like us and have the same problems as us and no other problems.

And that doesn't mean that sometimes immediate action isn't needed. But increasingly I'm assuming everything is complex, trying to learn not to take it personally if I'm wrong and not to be discouraged. I don't mind people laughing at me when I get it wrong. That's sort of my job. I can pretend it was something I said.

It's good practice anyway. I've two small children who will be 5 and 7 in 2023, so I will shortly be entering a decade and a half of being wrong about everything. I'll just wait for them to agree that I was right all along. But right now, I'd be happy to be 1 per cent less wrong than I was a couple of years ago.

Work/Life On Earth Balance

I think most people are sound and not assholes. Even sound people can occasionally be afraid, suspicious, susceptible to being manipulated, a bit lazy, slow to adapt to something new, shy about sticking their necks out, not want to look silly in front of their friends. They can be loyal to people around them, and dislike people they perceive as a threat, but not necessarily just because they are different. And, importantly, they might lack space/time/money to do the thing everyone says we all have to do. But they're mainly not dickheads. And they are people with jobs to do.

And, paid or unpaid, those jobs impact the planet in various ways. They might mainly be involved in typing or being on the phone or they might be responsible for what hundreds of acres of land looks like. They're just the jobs they do, and they may hate doing them or love doing them but, based on my Not Too Many Assholes theory, my hunch is that most people don't love their job because they love slapping the shite out of the natural world.

Since 60 per cent of Ireland is farmland, 11 per cent is forest and 16 per cent is bog, relatively few people have a lot of influence on a lot of nature. So they're going to get scrutiny. Maybe that seems unfair because they are producing things that all consumers use. There are relatively few diamond miners or superyacht builders in Ireland, but an ordinary punter in a fourth-floor flat in the Coombe can't do much about frogs on the bog, so it's better to ask the person on the tractor to help.

Farming is what I'm most familiar with. But growing up on a small farm, only helping out my father when he needed it, rather than actually having any responsibility, and then scooting off to Dublin for the Big Job means I know nothing about modern farming. I'd like to think I've a rough idea of how much I don't know. It's a bit like looking at an iPad and wondering where the floppy disk goes. If the iPad were enormous and needed dosing for mange mite.

So for now, I'm learning. I'm the interested townie reading farming articles, social media, listening to podcasts about beef weight gain (cattle, not mine) while being paranoid about commenting on something in case it becomes obvious I know significantly less than nothing about it. At times I find myself wading through climate-change denial shite, over-the-top hatred of anyone in the 'environmental lobby', but I have to bite my tongue because social media might look like it's connecting us but it's also specifically designed to encourage and harvest our hate like a ghoul (see 'Hey, why not use social media to connect? But also get the fuck off social media', page 234). Here's what I understand (by the way, I use quantitative terms like 'most' and 'a lot of' in the following sections – for an explanation of the statistical methodology, go to the section 'Statistical Methodology and Scientific Rigour in This Book' and you will find it doesn't exist).

I'd like to see you try it some time

Farmers work very hard. So do we all. And when they finish work, they worry very hard. So do a lot of us. But they're the victims of unforeseen circumstances like the bastarding hoor of a locking rear diff breaking for the third time this winter because the pins on the locking ring have sheared off and they're looking at a thousand euro at least. Big woop – machinery and tools break in a lot of jobs. Right, well, the weather can literally eliminate profits. Okay, some people have that challenge. But fewer. And a lot of farmers have animals or their crops can get disease. While I'm looking up the appropriate GIF to use to react hilariously to something on Twitter, they're on a Facebook group asking, 'Has anyone seen *this* before?' and it's a photo of a sheep with the largest scrotum you've ever seen. I'm shouting at the online banking because two-factor authentication is a pain while they're baffled at how a calf ended up stuck in the same drain twice in a half an hour. So farming is not like most jobs. So I understand when farmers get defensive, not because they are always in the right, but because I am at my most defensive if I'm being criticized while doing some manual work. Try it. Put your head under the sink to fix a pipe and get your head stuck, and while you're down there get someone to give out to you for your choices and how a new study says sinks should be fixed a different way. It doesn't mean farmers are automatically always right. They *could* be fixing the sink a different way – the carbon sink, amirite? – but I understand when they get annoyed.

I'm the bad guy?

For years they were told by the EU to make every single square inch of their farms produce grass or grain or food. Scrub is bad. Ditches only where absolutely necessary. Drain every single bit. The EU will pay you to do this. If you don't do this, you will be penalised. If you borrow to do this, you'll make the money back. And after 2010, this was also an act of patriotism. With the country's banks making such a hames of the place, the only industry growing growth as well as food was farming. Look at these legends making us proud! Our butter is the second most popular butter in Germany. IN GERMANY! (Please love us, Germany.) Now compare it to those smarmy suits playing accounting tricks with subprime loans and making an absolute *show* of the country. The farmers aren't into all that messing (apart from developers who started out as farmers, of course) – they're out in the muck and the shite. They're told to mind the bit of nature – like, don't be shooting eagles or anything, but don't be too worried about the dung beetles and the meadow pipits. Here's a few crap nest boxes under some kind of section 3234 green scheme. We need ye FEEDING THE WORLD. Because that's what Ireland does instead of borrowing from the world. Now, like Michael Douglas in *Falling Down* surrounded by crouching cops, they're saying, '*I'm* the bad guy?' standing next to a JCB and an enormous pile of limbs and scrubs and habitat that used to be on a ditch.

Also, think about when a green scheme comes in. Let's say you are a farmer paid to Do Something Green. Do you know how long will that money last? What happens when it runs out? A field that had a load of money-makers now has butterflies on it. In the summer. And what money there is is often tied up in the Way of Doing Things Now. In machinery and in land and materials. And land value. I love butterflies but I haven't paid money for them yet in my life. But you know that farms make food and food never goes out of fashion.

There are some jobs where you can feel and be told that you are making a difference – surgeon, lifeboat volunteer, comedian writing a book about climate anxiety. And growing food. It's part of your identity. Let's not pretend it's not a business – it's not loaves and fishes – but at the same time there is job satisfaction when you know you're making a real difference. Farmers do feel good about growing and raising food. From the small farmer to the P.J. Ewing on the ranch, their identity is linked to their job. Most people's jobs are part of their identity. But when you live on your job it's deeper. If someone told me my work was harmful, that I wasn't funny (they already do), a waste of space, I'd be upset and would not feel inclined to listen to what else they had to say. When you grow food and people tell you to make more room for nature and grow food less intensively, it's not wilfully ignorant to believe that less food will be grown and then to start thinking, *If I don't grow it who's going to grow it?* Yes, farmers want to make money, but I do believe there is a sense of mission there. There has to be – the hourly rate for a lot of them is too shite.

Farms often have a history, even if they've been consolidated into other farms. The land hasn't moved. There is memory there. Ties. Fellas getting into fights in pubs over fields. As they perceive it, people who wear scarves indoors are telling them what to do with their land. (Even if they don't actually own it, and they only have it leased, it's theirs by right – only someone was *got at* before making the will.) I'm telling you, the main inaccurate thing about the Bull McCabe was he was too open with his business – telling the whole pub what he was up to. But that's thespians for you. And the Yank was only planning to build a hydroelectric plant and quarry stone. Imagine if Tom Berenger was going to rewild the field.)

The word 'rewilding' can start people's eyes twitching. I used to love the word a bit more. Part of our farm at home is too steep and cornery to farm with big machinery. Dada used to plough it with the small Massey or it was grazed. Now it has turned back to nature. First it was farm-ugly – nettles and docks and thistles and then furze – but now creeping up through it are the oaks. Oaks, slow when you're watching them, but turn your back and they make headway. The hillsides look like a few millennia after the Ice Age finished. It's easy to fall in love with the idea of What If We Just Left It Be? It is lovely. But turning rural areas a bit wilder has a very dodgy lineage. A tradition of clearing people out to make a human-free paradise. For animals. Game ones and sheepish ones. I really don't think anyone is seriously proposing Highland Clearances, but sometimes that's the message that gets out there – that Bicycling Types want to clear the land for wolves so they can come and look at them sometimes while they're glamping. My own grandfather's birthplace is now a tourist attraction. I love Gougane Barra but it's poignant going there knowing people used to farm it. They weren't driven out of it by the aristrocracy with whips. The forestry service moved them to other land. I presume they were happy enough to go. But land is land.

Us and them

Farmers see, rightly and sometimes wrongly, their critics as urbanites who haven't an iota of what it is like to farm. 'Creative types' doing their campaigning on Twitter, or worse still in a book. They see themselves as scapegoats for everyone's problem. That feels slightly familiar to me. The pandemic, through no fault of my own, changed my job. One of my techniques which I needed to make money – talking to crowds in an enclosed space – was found to be bad so it was banned.

Well, imagine if it was banned for ever because there was no vaccine or it had to be done completely differently. Imagine I'd spent thousands of euro and a lifetime on a standup career that was totally based on sweaty indoor venues. Now imagine that the disease was sort of new, affected people in other countries more and mightn't affect people in the audience for twenty years, or only affect their children. I think I might be spending all day on Facebook calling scientists names too.

So what did help? The reason for my job being restricted was explained, I had a sense that we all had to play our part and I had to adapt. I lost income but didn't go broke. But the most important thing was I felt it was the right thing to do. Togetherness doesn't put bread on the table. That's why I got a bit of Covid dole, though. It's an imperfect analogy but I'd be surprised if there is nothing we can learn from the last two years about changing direction in a society. About what was done right and done wrong.

I really think that communication works both ways. Farmers, I know you feel battered by public opinion and are feeling defensive. Someone in an urban ivory tower said something in a statement that showed they don't understand your business. Okay! We'll deal with it after! We don't have time now! We need your help. You have to stop seeing every environmentalist and ecologist as plotting to take your land off you to give it to mysterious billionaire small-sunglasses-wearing vegans. I'm not saying it's not possible, I'm just saying that it's statistically unlikely. Do farmers honestly think that ecologists, environmental campaigners, water-quality testers, people who count birds are doing it for the money? There are so many ways of making faster money. People who love nature in this country are probably the only ones on a similar hourly wage and getting as much abuse as ye do. You have so much more in common. How many people do you think are doing it for the perverse pleasure of putting you out of a job? Do you honestly think they want you booted off your farm so they can depopulate the countryside like Teddy Roosevelt when he created the national parks? There might be a few sounding off on social media saying, 'Humans are an invasive species,' but I'm willing to bet there are acres of common ground between the ditches where farmers and others who care can find room for nature without anyone going bankrupt.

Change has to come. Something needs to be done. Nature in this country is hosed. There's no two ways about it. But biodiversity is having the shite slapped out of it all over the world. And Ireland is no different. That's not subjective. I know the wildlife might be fine where you are. But this isn't some complicated climate model. People are counting birds, mammals, fish, insects over the decades and finding there are less of them than there used to be. And so much of this damage has been done recently. Not just by farmers, but by foresters, roadbuilders, housebuilding (we've nearly twice as many gaffs in the country in the last generation), by the loss of bogs, those pricks who knocked gorgeous trees and ditches just so everyone could see their architect-designed bolthole-including-atrium from the road, river dredging, overfishing. But by acreage, farmers have the land; nature has disappeared and we need your help to put some of it back. We're not talking about going back to what it was like before Cromwell. If we could get back to the amount of wildlife around Italia '90, we'd be doing famously.

Amid the constant bad news about there being only three curlews left and two of them are planning to go to Berlin where it's cheaper, or yet more footage of thirty mature trees being cut suspiciously just before the nesting-season ban comes in because someone knows a fella with a saw that'll go mad if it's not used, I think there is still much to be optimistic about.

No better people

Just to do their normal job, farmers face a ridiculously wide range of challenges and have the skills to deal with them. They are often some combination of IT experts, vets, taxation and grant-application doyennes, midwives, mechanics, welders, carpenters, plumbers, inventors, nurses, ecologists, geneticists, renewable energy genera-tors, and, latterly, social media stars and campaigners. They own some of the biggest all-terrain machinery around, if machinery is what you need. They're called upon to help with flooding, Christmas lights, Big Funerals, charity events. I have never seen another profession that was so good at saying, 'Rightso fuckit we'll give it a go,' and going out and giving it a go,' They'll have a grove planted while I'll be composing the WhatsApp to our group about putting bedding plants next to a lamppost. I think it comes from having a bit of space. The average urban dweller – okay, me – mightn't have the space out the back to try something without someone ringing the council. So don't come to me to rewet the lower field. And many farmers know climate change is on the way. They worry about drought and floods and winds, about new pests in the field and new weevils in their tree-crop. They're fixing nitrogen all the time. I'm sure they'll fix carbon too. Time and time again, I see stories of farmers building miles of hedges, digging ponds, creating habitats for sand martins. There's a project in Mayo where they're growing patches of nettles as habitat for the corncrake. GROWING NETTLES? What demon has possessed them? But these are farmers who miss the *crex-crex* of the corncrake, a bird nearly extincted out of Ireland by modern grass management. And while they're at it, they're gently suggesting to people that, if you're going to make silage, mow from the inside out to give the animals a chance to flee to the ditches.

And speaking of ditches . . . Hedges hedges hedges.

Betting on hedges

We don't have Captain Planet to do quick rewilding. It'll take time, negotiation, a bit more knowledge. But we could start with hedges. If there's one thing we know in this country, it's hedges. Whenever I'm on the continent I get uneasy not seeing enough ditches in the countryside. It looks like chaos. If I was a livestock farmer in France, I wouldn't sleep at night. Cattle could wander all the way to the Caspian Steppes if they got out. But here they're going nowhere because of the ditches. It could be that 5 to 7 per cent of the land is ditches. If there were a county called County Hedge, it would be the fifth biggest in the Republic. Imagine that. One giant thorny, brambly county to hide in – a bit like Donegal.

When Dada came to Dripsey first, the farm had fourteen fields. Now there are five. He didn't make a prairie. He just made a 14-acre field out of six small ones. You couldn't blame him. The ditches weren't 20-foot walls of Eden. It was a few whitethorns and furze squatting on top of half-made old stone walls. Every year the cattle would scratch another cascade of stones out of the ditch and Dada had to keep on tidying and patching – eventually he got sick of that oul' shite. And he got an extra bit of acreage, which probably got him a small few bob from the Area Aid.

He's not the only one. Thousands of kilometres of hedge have been ripped up to make bigger fields, to let bigger machines turn and squeeze out a few extra acres. And when the electric fence came in we didn't need hedge for dividing up fields. Travelling on the train around Ireland you see piles of brush everywhere. The aftermath of a ditch massacre. And it's not done on the sly. YouTube is full of videos of fellas with giant machines sawing, digging, flailing the place to shite. And dead proud of it. People borrowing to get big tractors and cutting gear and then, to make them pay, hiring themselves out to the councils, and the councils get them to do the roads and no one asks them if they're biodiversity proof, and the place looks like some Marvel villain has been through.

There's still 700,000 kilometres of hedge left, which is enough to reach to the moon and back. But some of the hedge that's left might as well be growing on the moon because it's badly maintained, meaning the biodiversity is bad. The bottom of it is gappy. It's not doing much to stop soil run-off or reduce flooding. And it's not sequestering any carbon. And in a few years' time when we've stopped talking about Covid, we're all going to be talking non-stop about sequestering the carbon. It'll be small talk. How much are you storing? Have ye any room in yere's for a few kilos?

But if we don't look after the ditches, we'll have to store it in the attic or under the stairs.

So things will have to change. But they are, slowly. Whenever I'm feeling down, I watch videos of people *making* hedges and listen to podcasts of lads stomping around the country-side laying and talking about laying hedges. People who sound like Dada talking farming and biodiversity sense at the same time. Hedges reduce soil erosion; they provide shelter in heat and cold for animals. That's the beauty of hedges. They're not the only solution, but they're the one where we could all stand together – proper farmer, forester, even the likes of me – and learn how to weave a hedge. If done right, they're really good at storing carbon as well as wildlife. We're on the cusp of a hedge wave. I'd get in at ground level if I were you. Get some hedge funds together. I'm telling you, in 2023 the dryrobes will be in the attic and influencers will be filming themselves with billhooks, axes, bowsaws and loppers.

So make sure you get yourself a master hedge-layer who'll tell you where to put the hinge joints and what height. Preferably someone who is an All-Ireland hedge-laying champion. (Those championships exist, by the way.)

And in the meantime, as we flail around for other solutions, can we decommission some of the weapons? I'm just appreciating the beauty in the ordinary.

Call me by my name

Okay, I can't believe I wrote that sentence either. It's too . . . pure for the cynical likes of me. Too inspirational. But it's true. One of the biggest changes I've made recently has been to look at wildlife in this country differently. Growing up, I thought Irish wildlife was crap. I was fascinated by jungles and savannah. Big open spaces staffed by muscular, running, jumping, mauling, writhing, trumpeting, ear-flaring, stalking, dragged-to-the-bottom-of-the-lake-in-a-death-roll, buy-the-toy-in Hector Grey's PROPER ANIMALS. Mad bastard animals. I used to get these big thick library books by Willard Price, the Adventure series. *Amazon Adventure, South Sea Adventure, Underwater Adventure, Volcano Adventure, Whale Adventure, African Adventure, Elephant Adventure, Safari Adventure, Lion Adventure, Gorilla Adventure, Diving Adventure, Cannibal Adventure, Tiger Adventure, Arctic Adventure*. Hardbacks with smudged plastic covers over torn illustrated dust jackets and thick yellowed pages. The covers were lurid, usually showing a human being chased, walloped or strangled by a single-minded animal pertinent to the location. These adventures never featured Ireland. There was no badger adventure or clash with an ignorant bollox who kept bulldozing hedges in bird-nesting season.

I was shamefully dismissive of our wildlife. There just seemed to be too much of an emphasis on birds. Seals were good value but they weren't fighting the dolphins enough on Irish television. Any other mammal with a bit of bite seemed to mainly be targeted by people on horseback with hounds named after the animal. And that's just not fair. David Attenborough wouldn't deign to commentate on that.

Officially Ireland pays lip service to its nature. We are mainly interested in what visitors think of the place. We put out the good china and the coffee table books. For years, we assumed tourists love scenery. Tidy scenery. That's why we show them sweeping views of wild green windswept headlands around the coasts. Look how free you can be here. You can see forever. But you can see forever because a lot of it is a sheep-nibbled wasteland. We go to European countries, climb twice as high as our highest mountain and never wonder why they have trees up there when all we have is bits of heather. The one place we are always shiteing on about – the lakes of Killarney with its old oak forests where we've been extracting shillings from tourists for 140 years – is slowly dying because the oaks are ancient but there are none to replace them. It's either sheep- and deer-grazed carpet or rhododendron forest. There is no youth or succession policy. It'd be like boasting to the world about *Riverdance* but never replacing Michael Flatley.

So against that background, my little personal inspire-bollox is to respect the stuff we have. And the first step is to just know its name.

Nature is ugly and untidy and not colour-matched with our walls. It's not always the Serengeti with a cheetah slinking around like a supermodel or a three-way Royal Rumble between a wildebeest, a crocodile and a lion. Just like not all TV is Netflix-unmissable and you need the weather forecast as well, so it is that nature has its necessary, less glamorous parts. It takes a while to unlearn what we think about nature and wilderness. I blame the World Wildlife Federation for making the Giant Panda its logo. It's cuddly but it doesn't help itself, eating only bamboo even though its body clearly wants a bit of meat. I've heard it said it's a bit like the royal family. It's a freeloader but it brings in a lot of income. However, it means we only want cuddly stuff and not nettles.

During the lockdown in 2020, when the distance limits meant you needed a bit of imagination to bring some variety to exercise, I went on a good few cycles through industrial estates and other areas with spare land around them. I used to despair at the abandonment on the fringes. The half an acre here or there that could be a nice park with benches but instead has a dumped black bag at the edge. But beyond the edge – dumpers are arseholes but they're also lazy – you can see the weeds. And hear insects and birds. If you look at it a particular way, land neglect can be good.

Look at what's growing in the cracks in pavements in the more enlightened local authority areas. Of course the stripy-lawn merchants and the Kilgores who love the smell of

Roundup in the morning will give out about it. I would have been that way myself. I loved neatness. Dada loved neatness. But instead of complaining about it, just look more closely. The sheer amount of species you see is surprising. They're not giant flowers. They're sometimes a bit homely from a distance. They look a lot like . . . well . . . weeds.

And for a long time, I didn't even know what half of this stuff was called. All those pavement plants were still a mystery to me. I assumed they had two names: a Latin name like *Plantus plantypantus* and some colloquial name that reflects a store of old knowledge. A small pink flower called Housemaid's Elbow, Falconer's Umbrage, Saint Dominic's Preview, John-o-the-Hill-of-the-Hoor-with-the-Guzzy-Eye.

Well, I'm wondering no more. I have an app: PictureThis. PictureThis is now full of repeated mentions of very ordinary plants that I see growing in the corners and edges and ditches and derelict sites waiting for the price to go up around Dublin. Embarrassingly, I never knew the names of any of them before.

After that came the insects. I couldn't keep making up names for them. Although it is fun. I need to know the real names of the spudge-beetles, gonkflies and bloplice. I've started reverse-image-searching butterflies. I now know the names of four. I saw a peacock in Dripsey next to our regular primrose patch. Primroses that flowered in the same patch as long as anyone can remember. And now I'm onto birds. I don't have any photos so I've an app that listens to their birdsong and tells me what it might be. For a while, it was basically sparrows, because the fuckers wouldn't shut up.

But soon the swallows brrrrrrszzzzted into the conversation and then one day a goldfinch on the school-run. *Carduelis carduelis*, so good they named it twice.

* * *

When you name something you change how it's perceived. It won't save the hedges – people might still be more motivated by those sweet, sweet carbon-sequestering grants – but as the rest of us get up to speed and start to name the things around us, I think it can be a force for good. Normally I'm not one for quotes. It's tempting to find quotes that sound impressive but don't really match the thing you're talking about. Mandela once said in an address to schoolchildren that 'quotes are mostly bollox' but I like this from Robin Kimmerer in *Gathering Moss*:

It is a sign of respect to call a being by its name, and a sign of disrespect to ignore it. Words and names are the ways we humans build relationships, not only with each other, but also with plants.

6.

That wouldn't be
for me at all

'Plenty of fellas'd talk all right but when it'd come down to it, they wouldn't do a bit'

**– Dada on the nature of public
participation in A Thing**

Here in late 2022, we seem to be coming out the other side of the pandemic. This should be a time to get back to normal, with a sense of unity because we are all now free to *not* be in it together, which is unifying in its own way. We can do our own thing now. A society doesn't naturally cleave together during crisis like you'd think. Behind the headlines, there is plenty of grumbling during any wartime. For all the guff about blitz spirit, people in Britain were hugely traumatized by the air-war there. But they got on with it because there wasn't any choice. Just like we got on with it during the pandemic. We laughed at the fake WhatsApp voice notes about martial law. The endless walks. Arguing over who got to Mr Price for an outing.

There's no need for any more national effort or doing things on behalf of others. We are free to pursue our own individual ends.

But something feels wrong. It's like watching a Netflix show where they seem to have caught the murderer, but it's only episode six and there are ten in the series.

Something's not right. We're not finished. We're not even halfway through the prologue.

Because, assuming we're not also involved in a world war by the time you read this, as some of the worry of Covid dissipates, it's time to get back to worrying about the future again.

Worry begins at 40

It shouldn't be like this. I'm a forty-something male. These should be my glory years. Stretching out in front of me should be a lovely few decades of benign stagnation. Forty is a great age for two reasons.

Number 1: you are no longer under any pressure to achieve anything by a particular age. The whole culture of achieve-ment is skewed towards precociousness, the *hustle*, not letting the grass grow under your feet. It's reinforced every year in the media with various lists: 20 under-20 Leaders of Tomorrow, 30 under-30 Influencers, 40 under-40 Changemakers. You beat yourself up to achieve something by that age. You look at the list and think, *Well, it's okay – my birthday is in December, so I have six months to become CEO of a multi-million-euro business that fulfils contracts all over the world.*

But once you hit forty there are no more lists. No more pressure. You are on the list of 50 under-50 Not Bothering Their Bollox Getting Too Stressed About It Because They Won't Get the Thanks for It. Or 60 under-60 Leaving It Until Tomorrow Because the Day Is Gone. No one has set you a time frame for achievement, which leaves plenty of time for that other great thing about being over forty.

You are now welcomed into an exclusive club of people who can spend their time telling young people they have it easy and how tough it was in your day. You can leave comments underneath YouTube video of 1990s rap saying *For real, this is the shit. Original beats, real live MCs, none of the autotune shite. RIP TUPAC, ONE LOVE.* Even if you were living on a small farm in Dripsey listening to hip-hop recorded onto a TDK 90.

It should be a lovely time. A whole life of weaponized nostalgia stretching out in front of you. Assuming yourself better than the youth. Because they have it easy.

But all of that has been turned on its head. It's almost certain that generations to come will have it worse than us. And it's sort of our fault. How dare this happen? I put in all those years of work just so I could gently not give credit to future generations. That's the whole point. If I'd known, I wouldn't have put the time in. But now I realize that all the time I've been an adult, I've been a willing participant in putting my children and grandchildren in a position where their adulthood is uncertain.

This thought had been creeping up on me for a while, but in September 2019 I went to the school climate strike. I think I had always been aware in the abstract sense that climate change was a problem for young and future generations. But it hadn't hit viscerally. We often hand-wring about various issues and say, 'What kind of future are we creating for our young people?' We used to say it about the national debt. In the aftermath of the financial crisis, there was a lot of talk about the forty-something-thousand-euro burden on every single citizen. How we were borrowing money that our grandchildren would have to pay back. I thought, *Good. That'll soften their cough. They have it too easy, children.*

But this is different. Debt is a continuum. Climate is a cliff. And at the march, the abstract became tangible, standing there on Merrion Square in Dublin watching children protesting. Thankfully there was much to criticize in the young generation. I know for a fact some of them were dropped at the protest by their parents driving SUVs because the schoolchildren had neglected to install safe cycling infrastructure. I saw a lot of them using smartphones. How dare they be the first younger generation in history to be subjected to the half-a-trillion-dollar advertising industry and want essential consumer products? And the worst thing – plastic bottles of water. Have they not heard of imaginary drinking fountains that haven't been provided yet in Dublin? I was watching all of this having a good tut, as if the children had rolled there on a barrel of burning crude oil while bidding on NFTs with crypto, but the sheer weight of young people in all their wholesomeness just caring about the planet they live on brought me a moment of clarity: turns out you don't need to be a saint with thoroughly researched arguments and living a carbon-free life to make a valid point. In fact, it's impossible.

And even if that wasn't the case, children should still protest about stuff. Too many of us are sitting on our holes waiting. What else would you be doing as a teenager? Admin? Your VAT? And it's great for children. The excitement. Imagine what friendships start in protesting. There might even be a few shifts for the teenagers in unlikely pairings.

I am standing in the crowd, listening to the shouts and the hubbub. Like other parents of toddlers and scuttlers, we're 20 per cent engaged in the issue, 80 per cent on the lookout for threats: weather, strangers, out of control placards. But 20 per cent was enough to make it strike home. As I said earlier, I would cry at the drop of a hat. Watching children protest, I didn't have to wait for that hat to hit the ground. These children are not being manipulated by some mysterious kefir industrial complex. They mean it, just like you remember feeling strongly about anything as a child from roughly the age at which you could wipe your own arse. Imagine how capable you'd be at protesting a crisis on the planet. There's a girl up on stage doing spoken word. I look around at my children. They're a bit young for signs but around them are other children with signs saying 'There Is No Planet B'. There are other signs echoing Greta Thunberg – 'What are YOU going to do about it? You adults'.

I think about the future we've bequeathed them. What kind of a mess. They're getting stressed about our shit.

Now, we have fought some battles for them. My daughters will never have to spend ages stuck in a midlands town on the way to Cork – we built the motorways for them. Yeah, there's reproductive rights and marriage equality, but getting bypasses around towns was important too, you know.

And I take in this vista, the protesting children, the spoken word on stage, the faces of the children, my children, and I think, *my god, what have I done? They will one day be forced to do spoken word . . .*

NO, I'M JOKING – THAT'S NOT WHAT I MEANT!

People will be doing the finger-clicky thing instead of applauding . . .

NO, SORRY. What I mean is, this was a moment where I felt challenged to step up.

But before I step up, it's time to get over a few hang-ups.

Greta Thunberg and the way she might look at you

It's the Scandinavian thing, isn't it? Scandinavians always make us feel bad, with their cycling and their former prime ministers being reasonable after civil wars. And their public transport that works.

You go around Copenhagen or Stockholm and there are cyclists everywhere. Apparently operating without fear. It's not unlike going back to your primary school and seeing the children interact with the teachers in a friendly way, apparently unafraid of being hit or roared at. So it is in Scandinavia. Tootling along on old bicycles, like they have *rights as road users* or something. You might join them briefly. Rent a bike and feel a freedom and a lack of fear. When a motorist nears you and you immediately go into defensive position, they laugh Scandinavianly and say, 'No one will hurt you here.'

And it makes you more annoyed. This is how it could be. Why can't we have this? But instead of getting annoyed about the way it is here, we blame cyclists for crashing the lights that time.

They do it right in Scandinavia. Leaders in the world at everything. The bastards.

Whenever the news reports on some failing of government here, usually we are compared unfavourably to Scandinavia.

If Scandinavia lived in your estate, your mother would constantly be on the phone to you talking about her exploits. *The young girl of the Scandinavias is training to be a doctor. But they have brains to burn in that family. The mother was a lawyer and wasn't the father a diplomat? Don't I see him on the telly? Anyway, that's all my news. How's the job hunting going with yourself? Would you think of doing a course?*

I know I get annoyed when it looks like a European is looking at me dimly, with my prevarication and magical thinking and lack of taking responsibility. *I don't understand, Colm – why is there NO train serving any airport in Ireland? And why do politicians get raised onto shoulders when they get elected?* Ah, fuck off! I will defend our failings to the hilt and so I won't listen to you, Greta.

So if it's any consolation, the Scandinavians aren't all that. Sweden's not such a magical place. They're a bit racist and one of the ways they earn their money is by selling weapons that kill people. Suddenly Ireland selling everyone infant formula's not looking so bad, is it? And I see you, Norway. Aren't you amazing with your net zero? But it's not really net zero, is it, Norway, if you pay for it with shipping *400 squillion barrels of oil*? The money you're sitting on is filthy, isn't it, Norway?

And as for Denmark, well . . . I dunno. You have loads of pigs. I'm sure we'll find something.

So when Greta comes at us with her speeches, maybe that's it? When you with your bio that says 'Dad to Three Beautiful Daughters #bekind' posts some abuse about her, you just don't like being lectured by Scandinavians.

I mean, that shouldn't matter, should it? Or is it the parents? The father is an actor. The mother was in the Eurovision and came twenty-first, lost out to Johnny Logan. So they're definitely bitter about how much diesel Irish people burn. (Actually, she was in Eurovision in 2009, the year we didn't get to the final. See how easily fake news spreads when you have half the truth?)

But if that's the case, you don't have to listen to Greta. In fact, Greta wishes you'd stop listening to her and start listening to other young girls saying the same thing who come from all over the world.

Maybe listen to Vanessa Nakate, the Ugandan campaigner cropped out of a photo of climate activists, all of whom were white. She's worried that her country is getting too hot and too dry. Or the indigenous activists across the Americas who probably do more to reduce carbon emissions when they put their bodies on the line to block oil-sands pipelines than any wet-wipe in a beard getting his shoes and phone mended would ever manage in a thousand years.

Well, I'll tell you what my problem is. It's that *look*. Parents might recognize it. It's when a child gains enough sense to see through your bullshit. You get away with illogic and inconsistencies for a couple of years – *It's not nice to tell lies/ use bad words*. But then they start to notice the flaws. 'Daddy, why did you tell the lady I was three when you were buying the tickets? I'm not three, I'm four. Was that a lie? Was that a good lie or a bad lie?' 'Daddy, why did you shout a curse at that man on the bicycle when you were driving?'

And you're caught out. You mumble, 'Well, that was different.'

So when Greta is staring at us and saying, 'Why are you coming to me looking for solutions? I'm a child – you're the adults,' she's looking right through to our bullshit. Not you personally. At governments and multinational organizations, but it's still us. People our age. Those who stood idly by.

And I could get defensive and say, *Don't be telling me about sustainability, Greta. I grew up in the eighties and had only two jumpers, and we ate food way past its best-before date.*

To which she could equally reply, *And then what happened? If you were so sustainable in the eighties why did the pace of destruction and carbonization explode after 2000?*

I'll have to get back to you on that one, Greta. We took our eyes off the ball and now we have to do a bit of work.

Talking Rubbish

But I *was* doing work. I just wasn't sure where it was going.

As I inched towards the age my father was when I had my earliest memories of him, I started to slowly take on some of his habits. His pronunciation of a cough (*mmBLEUGH-HHamm*); telling people 'these trousers will see me out'; calling every passing dog by the name of a dog we had in the 1990s; and these days, every now and then, picking up other people's rubbish.

Maybe my father started doing it to prevent the cows eating Tayto bags that had been thrown over the ditch, but then it became a by-product of his Walk. He'd walk along the boundaries of the fields to see what people had thrown out of their cars. Most of the time he returned muttering darkly about chip bags. Sometimes he found a pint glass or once, weirdly, a clock made of slate that worked perfectly. Literally someone wasting time.

I watched him doing this year after year, the inability to walk past rubbish lying on the ground, and it built up that impulse till it eventually spilled out in my finding myself, one evening, in a parish hall near where I live in Inchicore in Dublin, at a meeting to Do Something about the Litter.

If you've ever been to a meeting to do something about a thing, there is first a phase where people get to talk about how bad the thing is. But then someone will say the fateful words, 'So what are we going to do about the thing?' Most people are shy, so a silence will follow, broken by nervous laughter and someone saying, 'Well, that's the million-dollar question.' Eventually, like some sort of reverse gravity, hands will start rising almost of their own accord.

There's nothing mystical about what raised my hand. Others were doing the same. But let's pretend Dada appeared in a vision, so we'll go with 'not wanting to let my father down'.

Either way, after that meeting, I was one of the People of the High-Vis. And proud to don the uniform. It's one of the simple inventions that changed the world. A bit like the pneumatic tyre perfected by John Dunlop – and sure what else would he invent with a name like Dunlop? – or the paperclip, the washing machine, the screw or the USB port on the back of tellies that allowed you to charge your phone in a hotel if you forgot the plug bit and reception only had a hundred entangled Nokia chargers.

So thanks to Bob Switzer from California, who started messing with fluorescent chemicals and eventually invented day-glo paint for fabrics: the high-vis. And the rest, as they say, is local history. Because it's not just the garment we take for granted: it's some of the people who wear it – the volunteers.

To see the high-vis in all its glory, it's best to travel the back roads. The roads where there is a litany of Local Events – charity runs, road bowling, religious processions, matches, commemorations of armed insurrection. And at each one, the same friendly faces, the robust optimism and altruism of the guerrillas of the People's High-Vis Front.

That meeting was ten years ago. Since then I'd been doing a small bit along with a group of neighbours. We supported each other. We gave out about things together. There was solidarity. We shared the same murderous vigilante thoughts.

The murderous thoughts are mainly caused by two things: dog turds left in small black bags tied to a tree and broken glass.

In the pantheon of Small Stupid Shit Humans Do, is there any more annoying a thing? You bring your dog for a walk, you are attentive enough to bring a bag, you are tolerant of smell and texture enough to package up the hellish Play-Doh into a small black drug-deal bag and then . . . you stop. You leave the bag and walk away. Or, weirdly, you tie it to a tree. Like the turd of your three wishes or an offering in a pagan grove to your ancestors. It's actually worse than leaving the shit out there, in the open air, to biodegrade. If you're going to the trouble of tying it to a tree, fuck it, put a choc-ice stick in it for visibility so at least we know there are improvised faecal devices around the place. Let the worms and woodlice and slugs and flies and pigeons-with-a-kink have a go at it. At least the nightsoil returns to the soil. And there's the broken glass. The most clichéd sign of urban decay. I respect your right to drink from a glass bottle in the summer weather. But you should know that glass is the ultimate malevolent entropy in the universe. An intact bottle is benign; it has no nefarious uses. It can be a container, an ornament, a musical instrument.

But a broken one. It hurts dogs – the same ones whose shit never fulfilled its natural destiny, and now they've a cut paw. What a dog-day afternoon! It hurts children. Just one broken bottle and your estate is being used for a Ken Loach film. Can I make a plea? If you see a craftily stored glass Hooch bottle next to the wall beside a traffic-light switching box, can you put it somewhere an asshole won't break it?

I had good days and bad days out picking rubbish. We reunited a canal bike (a bike dumped in the canal, not a pleasure-craft hybrid) with a distraught 12-year-old owner who'd had it robbed from him. And new volunteers would join and feel part of something. But equally there would be a day when we'd find a bag of grown-up nappies in the water that was too heavy to lift out without a crane and we'd just think, *How could you dump nappies in a canal? How could that be a thing you'd choose to do?* It'd make you despair. I tried to understand their motivation and the stress they might be under but that was doing no good. So instead I had a fantasy where I was an avenging vigilante who watched the canal from the shadows, lit only by the glowing ember of my cigarette, waiting for the tell-tale splash of a dumper. Ready to strike.

It felt thankless and I think I was doing it for thanks too. A powerful drug. I lived for it, picking up rubbish and staring people down – *Thank me, why don't cha?* – in the hope that they'd say something, that I'd get a *Fair play*.

And then sometimes a weird relationship develops. Like between me and Linden Village man. There's a man – I'm guessing it's a man. He drinks Linden Village, smokes Pall Mall and eats lots of sliced ham – who dumps about one bag of rubbish every two days, perfectly tied in the same ditch near the canal. And about once a month I bring his twenty bags to the council depot. He basically has a personal waste disposal butler. We never see each other. In a weird way I've stopped being angry about him. He's not chaotic. The bags stay intact. It takes me about 20 minutes to de-dump them. A couple of times he's been late restarting the dumping and I get worried about him. Is he okay? His routine is off. And then one morning I'll see the tell-tale black bundle behind a tree. Am I doing a good thing that's just a bit pointless, or even worse, is picking up rubbish a distraction? Greenwashing? Making it look like something is being done while the world burns? That's the hardest thing to admit being wrong about. What if doing something is worse than doing nothing? And the whole concept of picking up litter has murky beginnings. Round about the 1950s the plastics boom was taking off in America. People were being told to use disposable everything. Advertising for decades said things like 'In this disposable age, is there a reason for the non-disposable bottle?' 'Get this plastic cup at Toss-away prices.' High-quality plastic was replaced by throwaway. 'Say goodbye to washing up.' They were told to throw it away and not save it. So people threw it away. In huge amounts. And people started to notice the rubbish piling up along the highways and in the rivers. But rather than encourage reusable or durable materials, the packaging and beverage industries were worried that the rubbish would lead to laws reducing packaging. So they deflected the attention from them to the consumer. Among general sneakinesses, they backed – not publicly – the Keep America Beautiful campaign. This campaign, among other things, made a short film featuring an Italian actor playing an Native American for a video campaign in the 1970s that guilt-tripped and lambasted Americans for clogging up rivers with the trash they had previously been told to throw away.

We wouldn't fall for that kind of rubbish here, would we? No, of course not. Although the Tidy Towns was sponsored by a company that sells water in plastic bottles. But that's different: it's not as if you can just turn on a tap to get waterrrr. . . Anyway, leaving that aside, when you add up the feelings of guilt, when trying a bit feels futile, it might just be easier to hide, mightn't it?

Nowhere to run

But you can't hide from this thing. The story will find you. Once you know you can't unknow. Bad news will find you unless you switch everything off and go to live in the woods. Eventually the stories will winkle you out. You'll be out hunting sustainably managed feral hogs and someone will whisper, *You know keep-cups are just as bad for the environment, don't you? You have to use them a few hundred thousand times but you don't. You keep getting free promotional ones, don't you?*

You'll be meditating and someone will WhatsApp you about olives being hoovered off trees – wait, what?

Yes, up until quite recently, millions of migratory birds died each year in the olive harvest in the Mediterranean. I wasn't even looking for olive fatalities when I came across this headline. It turns out most olives aren't harvested by hand by a twinkly-eyed Grandad Jose from his thousand-year-old tree that knew the Moors. He doesn't dispense wisdom about the futility of possessions as his oaken fingers caress nature's bounty. THEY'RE HOOVERED OUT OF THE TREES BY GIANT HOOVERS. And until recently, they did it at night for extra freshness. And do you know who else is in trees at night? Birds. Hoovered. Just so you could have olives in little ramekins for the people who turned up for the party early when you weren't ready.

They fixed it in 2020 and no longer harvest at night. But I had to go looking for that news. In the meantime I was cry-eating the olives.

Every time I read about taking a step in the right direction, that step was actually to trample a rare gannet's nest. Greenways are good? Not if they're cutting down trees to bring us closer to nature. The plastic-bag tax – that had to be good, right? Yes definitely but now we're all buying these organic cotton bags that use a squillion times more water and land and . . . AAARRGGHHHHH!

Since running away wasn't an option, and accidentally reading bits here and there seemed to bring only pinpricks of guilt and despair, I decided to embrace the disaster. I started from the nihilistic view that if, one day, I ended up minding my grandchildren in the barren wasteland of a climate-changed world while their parents were out searching for edible roots, at least I'd be able to look them in their tear-stained eyes, and when they asked what did I do, I could say I did marginally more than nothing.

That's an artificial starting point. It's also probably bullshit. The wasteland is already happening to millions of people around the world and I didn't do anything to prevent that.

But sometimes you need a bit of bullshit as a starting point. I think of it like in mathematics where you assume some stuff to get you started and go back and refine after. (I'm not a mathematician. But I like to assume I am to get started.)

I embrace the shit but don't wallow in it.

I decided to read more and listen more. It sounds counterintuitive to consume more bad news. I would have thought the more I knew, the more depressed I'd get. For a start, there is only so sad you can get about bad news until eventually you're full and it can't do any more harm. But it has actually given me some comfort. I'll explain.

A hundred companies produce 70 per cent of emissions. To be fair, they don't do it laughing villainously at lavish CO_2-extravaganza parties (well, most of them don't). They do it making stuff to move/feed/heat/entertain/kill/shelter humans. But also by chasing profits and keeping shareholders happy, and if share prices go up then a small number of CEOs get a ridiculous salary. Also by 2030, the richest 1 per cent of people will be emitting 16 per cent of the carbon emissions. Clearly much of their consumption will have to be luxury because they don't have stomachs sixteen times bigger than everyone else or need to be sixteen times warmer. That stat could cause despair at the futility of getting my shoes mended. I could just throw my hands up and cut the crusts off my bread and throw them away out of spite. Even though I love crusts. But on the flip side, it shows if a relatively small number of people change, that could change a lot. And therefore it's counterproductive to blame 'the rest of humanity' as a fundamentally sick species who just deserves the apocalypse. (A fatalistic view that says, 'I can't wait until we're extinct and the animals frolic among the decaying rubble of civilization once again.' Which would be fine except there'd be no one to monitor the nuclear power stations and eventually they would melt down and that'd put a stop to all the frolicking.) Most people emit the carbon they emit and consume the resources and nature they do just to provide the basics with a few treats. (What the basics are in each country varies, obviously.) So getting angry with them is pointless. But encouraging them to be actively interested in what the Mr and Mrs Bigs are up to is not pointless. Nor is communicating in a clear way about how changing how you do things might not mean unbearable hardship.

Which brings me back to the System. Personal responsibility and washing out your yoghurt cartons for the recycling is one thing. But eventually you realize that the entire way of doing things for centuries has been based roughly on dig it, burn it, drive it, dump it. I don't know how different things would have been if we were more 'When we eat the bison we give thanks because we respect it.' Would we still have Bluetooth earphones and Snapchat filters without destroying nature? Why not? But, ultimately, our economic system and measurement of worth are still rooted in To Hell With the Planet. It's really hard to change that, and it takes a lot of people to want it so the people who can actually make the change feel they have no choice.

This doesn't mean I as an individual should do nothing. I've just chosen to take it to mean, *If I'm a massive hypocrite and get things wrong and initially do more harm than good and never make more than a marginal contribution, it's still not a reason not to try.* That simple 'keep going' message is what I tell myself every time I see someone cut a hedge with a machine from *Mad Max: Fury Road*.

But it's fucking hard to even comprehend the enormity of what needs to be done. So I'm trying hard to learn how to be comfortable wallowing in complexity. I desperately wanted to know about simple solutions, to identify the clear bad guys. It's uncomfortable when you realize people have understandable reasons for doing what is perceived to be the wrong thing. Because you then have to do a bit more learning. It's fun to lean against the mantelpiece at a party, five cans deep, and hold forth on how they just need to 'rewild the fuck out of it'. It's not as fun to hear nuance. It's not fun to hold a project back because some consultation needs to be done or some tests or regulations or paperwork or I's dotted and T's crossed. But that's the least we half-arsed Johnny-come-latelies can do. For years eco-warriors and campaigners and researchers and scientists and engineers and artists and all sorts have been campaigning and shouting and even, in 2022, chaining themselves to gates and, in one case, burning themselves alive, desperately trying to wake people up about this. They weren't tree-huggers or anarchists or communists or Wiccans or lefties or liberals or trustafarians – or not all of them, and if they were, *so what*? By and large they were right. Even if we're not camped out in the woods chained to a tree, the least we can do is be aware.

The more you read the more likely you are to come across information that motivates you in your own personal work. For example, I learned that 80 per cent of ocean litter comes from the land. Which means that when we pick up rubbish in our little area between a canal and two rivers, there's a mathematical chance we are preventing that Hunky Dorys bag and bottle of energy drink from wrapping themselves around a turtle's intestine. Just a small chance, but a chance nonetheless. Something that elevates our work above point-less. And that's all I need to do – literally anything. A drop in the ocean is still one drop more than none (I have a very low pointlessness threshold).

Eventually, no matter how much I read or hear or how much bad news I consume, I can't get any more miserable, so the Law of Diminishing Shite comes into play, where each successive bit of bad news has less incremental effect on me. Eventually I just think, *Ah well, the sun will eventually turn into a white dwarf and incinerate us in five billion years.* But when you hear good news, no matter how small, it packs a punch. It's a strong pleasure – like eating crackers and cheese standing up. You can't get enough of that. Like, for example, since 2010, indigenous activists campaigning against oil and gas pipelines across their lands – pipelines which would often carry dirty tar sands and fracking projects – have prevented up to one and a half billion tons of carbon emissions. Ireland emits sixty million tons a year. It's not all Hollywood. Sometimes it's people putting their bodies on the line.

Networks, networks, networks

When I first started picking up rubbish in the area, I knew maybe a handful of people. The butcher, the baker (fella in the chipper), the candlestick maker (or at least the person who lit the candles in the restaurant). There was no sense of ownership of the public spaces. If I saw something annoying, I fumed and swore I'd email someone sometime and then never did. But now . . . eh, well, sometimes 'something gets done'. There are up to a hundred of us who at least know each other to say hello to, who at some stage over the last few years have spent at least ten minutes emailing, talking, picking, planting, gossiping, drinking tae, eating biscuits, more gossiping and sending silly jokes on WhatsApp with each other. We are from, at last count, maybe ten countries – and that's not including culchies. It's unstructured at times – there aren't five-year goals or strategic visions yet. It's messy and fun and frustrating and then fun again. And it mostly started with picking up rubbish.

Litter-picking is a sort of a gateway drug into thinking about other environmental issues. Anyone can pick up rubbish. No report is going to come out saying you're actually harming red grouse by removing their source of discarded curries. So it's an early success to get you hooked on doing something. You get to meet other people who all fall under the vague category of Giving a Shit. People from all backgrounds and ideologies and attitudes. People who have diverging views on lots of things like weeds, energy, electric cars, cycling, bogs, farming and food. People who would be tearing lumps out of each other on social media. But they all roughly agree that empty Monster Munch packets in a canal are a bad thing. And you will have disagreements with them on how to do the right thing, and they'll know more than you, and you'll be wrong about something and find out you're accidentally a massive hypocrite about something. But you have the rubbish in common. The rewilding plan didn't work when a lad with a mower cut all the yellow rattle? Chin up, remember when we cleaned up the playground together? We'll start again. We'll do the boring stuff about finding out how private contracts are awarded to managing public ground.

And when we do a bit in the public space, it gives us confidence to email about this, to petition about that. I've emailed actual elected representatives! I haven't had this many dealings with government representatives since I was using spare election posters to paint *2000 AD* characters as a child. But now I'm easily settling into the role of Polite Pain in the Hole, emailing who I think might read and respond. And each year we inch forward on something and try not to take setbacks personally.

I now understand a tiny fraction of what it is to manage waste for a living. I've an awful lot more understanding of the workers – private and public – who have to pick up other people's shite. Especially being treated as invisible. Most people ignore me, apart from the odd person asking if I'm doing it as community service to avoid jail. 'Yes, it is my community service, my friend,' I say in an Aslan-the-lion voice. 'But no one's ordering me to do it.' I don't really. You can't be doing Narnia voices around Inchicore.

I can't quote magical Erin Brockovich results where I give a speech and Colm's Law is passed whereby Dogshit in a Tree people are strung up in the very trees they'd previously decorated. No. My mantra is very much 'Support, not condemnation'. Or 'Scaffolding, not the scaffold'. It's hard to measure our progress in terms of tons-of-shite-per-square-yard reduction. But you can measure it in trees planted, a park refurbished or metrics like Amount of People Who Know Each Other, or Length of Time a Mattress Stays Dumped Before It Is Picked up By the Council.

Should we actually be protesting more? I'm not really good at proper activism. Yet. I don't know what I'm good at, really. Or I hadn't thought about it until I heard one other vital titbit shortly after I started properly seeking things out.

Three circles and a bit in the middle

One of the things I started listening to was a podcast called *How to Save a Planet*, which outlines various facets of the World's Biggest Problem. One of the co-creators is Dr Ayana Elizabeth Johnson, a marine biologist, author and policy expert. The podcast is extremely listenable and has plenty of podcasty 'Oh. I. Did. Not. Know. That.' moments. But frequently Dr Johnson talks about how people come to her asking her how they, just one person, can help, given how big the problem is.

Asking an eminent person 'How can I be better?' is one of the oldest questions in the book. Or in The Book. In the Bible a young man came to Jesus asking how to get into heaven, and Jesus told him to sell all his stuff, give the money to the poor and follow Jesus. And the young man said, 'AH, C'MON, LIKE!' (I'm paraphrasing). I've never identified with anyone in a Biblical setting more. THAT'S TOO HARD.

Dr Johnson has come up with something that helped me get started. I'm not saying it will lead me to renounce everything, but it helped me to frame what I'm already doing and stop wasting time feeling bad about what I'm not doing.

She says to ask yourself three questions. First, what do you love doing? What brings you joy? You need a bit of joy in the job, otherwise it'll be a miserable slog, given the size of it.

Second, what are you good at? What are your special skills from work or play or hobbies? What are your networks? Who do you know because of where you're from, where you live, the clubs you're already part of?

Third, what needs to be done? Well, obviously everything. But is there an area where you can say, 'Right: that needs doing now.' Something you can influence? One where there might be a chance of success that will give you the confidence to do the next thing? I mean, you *could* start with coral-bleaching. Definitely. Likewise, I would not dissuade anyone from fighting poachers. But for a start, is there something nearby?

Then the simple suggestion from Dr Johnson is to make a Venn diagram of those three questions, and the bit in the middle is where you could start.

So, money, mouth and the placing thereof. What about me? What's my Venn diagram? It looks a bit like this.

What do I love doing?
- Eating biscuits and falling asleep while reading
- Letting people turn right and getting a wave
- Reading about insurance claims and getting angry
- Guessing the size of jars for leftovers
- Being liked   • Cycling   • Gossip   • Words
- Picking up rubbish

* What I should do

What needs to be done?
- EVERYTHING
- People need to feel part of something
- People need to laugh
- People need to know
- People need to talk about it
- People need to see the joy in it

What am I good at?
- Guessing the size of jars for leftovers
- Not good at conflict so I get on with people
- Not good at principles so I get on with people
- Low expectations and high pain threshold. *Maybe I love the misery*
- Seeing where people are coming from
- Picking up rubbish   • Making people laugh
- Bringing people together (in small groups)
  - Spreadsheets
    - Writing polite emails

What do I love doing?

I love making people laugh. Pure and simple, that moment where you drop a punchline, the confounding of expectations, the juxtaposition the listener isn't expecting, the realization on their face, watching them take big lovely breaths of air. But humour generally works best when it's puncturing pomposity; absolutely lambasting hypocrisy; breaking the rules; punching up; the underdog, the set-up and the surprising outcome. But unfortunately for humour in this situation, it can also be about pulling down one's trousers in the face of earnestness and the need to do the right thing. What would be funnier than this entire book would be if I went on a long impassioned rant about how we live on a planet that is a miracle of the universe and we should look after it, then there was a pause and you just farted. Even funnier because you produced emissions. If I said we need to help other species of bees and you said Bees Me Hole and made the Wanker Gesture. That's just funnier. Green stuff just isn't very funny. Cos, like, you know, we might all be spiralling into hell. But that's the challenge. And a joke that works even when it's hard is all the sweeter. It sounds naff as hell, but laughing at a joke that has some bit of an idea in the payload would be lovely to me. It doesn't always land. You can see when an audience feels like they're being preached at. Especially an Irish audience. *Ah, shag off with your message.*

I'm nosy. I like to find out about people. I get that from Dada. Dada was a talker. But he didn't go on. He let other people go on. He'd come back from a walk late and say, 'So-and-so kept me talking.' But what happened was so-and-so kept answering your gentle open questions, Dada. He was about to go when you said, 'Tell me who's building that house over next to Murphys'.' I'm interested in people's stories. (Except when I'm picking rubbish. I'm a lone wolf there. A soldier of fortune, a man with no name, haunted by what I've seen: the dogshit, the nappies, the medical and self-medicating waste.)

I like the power of a well-chosen word, a good old-fashioned curse word in the right place. I'm fascinated by why how a message is delivered and who delivers it make such a difference. What went wrong? What went right? I'll get it wrong in this book, I'm sure, and I hope I'll be adult enough to take it on the chin even though it's just people saying stuff because they're only pure jealous. I really like trying to explain things to people (this needs to be watched). I like plans. I like to see where a thing is going.

What am I good at?

Asking a comedian who majors in self-deprecation what's he good at is going to lead to a lot of football-interview-type responses. *Well, look it, it's not about me – it's about the team at the end of the day, and if I'm just a useless slug, a barnacle on the team ship, and don't get in the way, I'll be happy.* So it's easier to start with what I am not good at. I'm risk averse and seem to spend too much time worrying about public liability insurance. I once worked on a small local concert. I was on a committ*EE*. Comedy has made an industry of slagging committees. Now, I was poacher-turned-Poacher-Committee-member. One of the other people was a big thinker who came up with the con-cept and went with it. But I was slow and wanted detail. I realized quickly that if everyone there was like me, there would be no concert. But once a thing is up and running, I'm good at worrying and to-do lists in spreadsheets. Every project should have someone who is afraid everything is going to go wrong. But don't give them too much power.

I want everyone to like me. I don't like conflict. I grew up in a house where my mother and father exchanged approximately fifteen cross words that I heard, per year. I don't know what to do in a row. I freeze. I'm slow to protest, to attract attention to myself, in case people laugh at me in a bad way. I'm shit at 'debating'. I see everyone's side. Put me in a room with a reason-able person from the Owns Enormous Pickup Truck for No

Good Reason Except Has Insecurity About Size of Willy lobby and I'll immediately admit I'm wrong. On the flip side of that, I might be good at minor acts of diplomacy. And recognizing that not everyone is in a position to help in the same way or to the extent you're helping, but that doesn't mean they don't care.

I'm good at drudgery. A long, repetitive task is fine by me. Tell me what to do and I'll do it.

What needs to be done?

Apart from everything? But in order to do everything we need people to work together. The environmentalist Rob Hopkin said *if we wait for governments it will be too little too late, if we act as individuals, it'll be too little; but if we act as communities, it might just be enough, just in time.* Like all quotes, it's a summary. It's not the whole story. They are sort of intertwined. And also there are enormous companies that need to act. If we wait for politicians to do something, we'll be too late. They're no different to us in many ways. They have a mix of altruism and self-interest. They are not any more likely to be noble, so they'll wait for people to demand something. But they won't always lead. If you do it by yourself, it won't be enough. If you work in a community, and from there challenge bigger entities to do more, that's our best chance. So we need connections. We need networks of like-minded and unlike-minded people. We need people who know each other. They don't need to agree on everything. They just need to give a shit.

So what am I doing?

My own personal bit: the six Rs – refuse, reduce, reuse, repurpose, recycle, replant a few trees – yeah, grand. It's piddly. But that's just the stepping stone. It gives me confidence, helps reduce hypocrisy by 4 per cent, so maybe gives me a small bit more credibility, and sets an example for the two children. That's private (apart from putting it in this book), but my nosiness, wanting to be liked, reasonable amount of awareness of social cues, being handy enough at typing and painfully slow at phrasing, mean I might be good at introducing people to each other. Creating networks, finding common ground between people. Sensing when others are pissed off. So it still comes back to picking rubbish, sort of. The gateway and the networks it helped to start. And, gradually, learning on the job, branching out from there. And the nosiness about how things happen in my local area. And how we talk to one another. Because we are wasting *so* much time shouting from inside tents. And we don't have time to waste.

So I'll try and give people a laugh. The news is grim. People who work trying to turn the tanker of an economy around to not destroy what's left of nature and change the atmosphere, literally and metaphorically, might like to laugh about their jobs and All This Shit too. And maybe other people will come along who are just curious. The laughs have to be about more than *Do you remember penny sweets, do ya? What was all that about?* Introducing ideas, having an audience at a gig who wouldn't normally get on or agree but might laugh at the same joke from different angles. Then after the show they get drunk in the bar and hug it out.

Because that's what always happens at the end of films. These are all lofty aims but what harm? You won't have a loft without a ground floor. (Okay, sorry, it's these quotes. They're making me *too* inspirational.)

For now that's my start. Networks and laughs and probably some spreadsheets. What are you good at, what do you like to do and what needs to be done? You can't have my one. Environmental comedy gigs are hard enough to sell without competition. Stay in your lane. But there are any number of lanes. And you don't need to be all nicey-nicey and collegial all the time. The movement needs a few bolloxes as well. People who don't need to be liked as much. People who can throw a few FUCK-OFFs into a situation. But only where appropriate. Please consult with the media team first. So are you A Bit of a Bollox and Proud of It? Your planet needs you.

7.

Won't somebody think of the children?

'As the fella said, it'll be all the same in a hundred years'

– Dada, regularly, when faced with an intractable problem

Note: The following may contain traces of doting and 'AH, WUDJA LOOK?' in relation to small children. But this chapter is not exclusive to those who have personally parented children. If you've minded, grandparented, honorary/by marriage or biologically aunted/uncled/ piblinged a child or are generally positively predisposed to people who are quite young and the children they might have in future, it's for you too. Inevitably, I may stray into assuming everyone is a parent or wants to be, but I promise I will never wittingly go full-blown, condescendingly head-tilty *You see, if you were a parent you'd understand.* My editor has been instructed to watch out for this and turn on the power to the electrodes to zap me out of it.

Anyway, where was I? Ah, yes. I suppose it was when I became a father that I really understood the preciousness of life. Where my dads at? Right? It's only then I really knew empath–*BZZZZZT!* Sorry (thanks, editor).

But I do look at them, my kids. Nibbling a cracker on a bench after a walk. Their little faces, with the noses and eyes and – *squeee!* – little hands. It is extraordinary to observe people who are so free from major worries. I'm not saying they live in the moment and that the moment passes. They are extremely goal-oriented. If lollipops have been promised, that promise is entered in a ledger system that they both can access. It's a little cloud-based local network. They won't forget that promise. They are extremely focused on birthdays: their imminence and what things they might get for them. But they're not *worried*. They are lucky – there are children all over the world who do have deep worries. I am grateful that mine don't, and I'm not sure I should inflict any worry on them.

But first, the conversation I won't be having with my children: should we have had them?

Having them in the first place

Well, obviously we should have. Just look at them. Here, look, I've a photo of them on my phone. Have you ever seen such a pair of absolute dotes–? *BBZZZZZT!*

There are nearly eight billion people in the world, and it'll go up for another thirty or forty years at least. The rate of growth has slowed but that's still a lot of people. More people need more food, water, heat, stuff. And the planet isn't getting any bigger, so obviously that's going to impact the climate and all the other animals living here. But if you focus on saying over-population is the problem, it isn't long before, with the best will in the world, you'll find yourself – not you, oh no, just others in the conversation – saying where there seem to be too many people living. The over-population is rarely the housing estate in an Irish flood plain or the city in the Californian desert. It's other places that need to cop on a small bit. More foreign ones.

And it's not like the sheer number of people on the planet and the animals and farmland needed to feed them isn't a problem. And one thing's for definite: we can't all continue consuming the same amount of energy/land/shit processed meat/stuff we're doing right now. But if you find yourself chatting about this with someone and the conversation seems to be an awful lot about how many children people in poorer countries are having, then you're faced in the wrong direction. (One of the nine countries that will account for most of the population growth before 2100 is the USA, but there's a strong chance they'll mention somewhere poorer and 'foreign-er'.)

If, on the other hand, your conversation really focuses on how to support countries to stop child marriage and forced marriage, to improve women's education, rights, access to contraception and maternity leave, and to provide social security – if *that's* what they're getting at in the comments section underneath a story about the loss of mangrove

swamps, then they are correctly talking about over-population as a symptom of inequality, rather than the main cause
of climate change. Because not all people are doing the same
amount of climate changing.

The carbon footprint of someone living in a rich country
like, I dunno, Ireland is about eighty times that of a poorer
country, like Niger, which has one of the world's highest
birth rates. Which means that each baby born in Ireland
does way more carboning than one in Niger, and it really
doesn't matter how many children are in the family there.

Carbon footprint is not a perfect measure of what an individual might be doing. Not everyone in Ireland is in a patch
of carbon-emitting degraded bog or a data centre. It's an
average. But equally, not everyone in Niger is a subsistence
farmer who plants, grows and harvests cashews or high-
quality cocoa or cycles to an office job. Some work in the
uranium or cement industries.

This book is not sophisticated enough to work out the
weighted, all-things-considered difference between the
(very) average Irish and Nigerien comedian, but I'm going
out on a limb and suggesting I'm burning way more hydro-
carbons and releasing way more carbons than they are.

I definitely burn gas in the boiler and diesel in the car. The
average Nigerian whimsical author trying their hand at a
serious topic might have a gas boiler (or air conditioner) but
statistically could more likely be cooking with kerosene or
even carbon-neutral biomass. I'm seventy times more likely
to have a car than they are. I hope their gigs are nearby.

So assuming my two adorable little super-emitters are the same as me throughout their lives – perhaps burning less diesel, but carbon-wise – the agent of over-population is still me and my small family.

Would it be better if countries had better education so women were more in charge of how many children they'd like to have? Yes, but before you comment, can I see your qualifications to talk on this subject and the work you have done on women's rights in the Global South? If you have none, I suggest we both take a step back from lecturing others about family size. Let's not pretend we weren't having loads of children in Ireland, oh, about forty years ago. And it's only since doctors stopped asking for a letter from the priest to get a bit of contraception that the numbers have come down.

But what about biodiversity? Aren't they always going around with giant bags of sticks on their backs for the fire, like I saw on the news that time, the time the news anchors arrived in Niamey for That War About Scarce Resources? They'd turned an area into a desert with their inefficient wood stoves, whereas I turn on a tap and gas comes out and I don't cut down any baobab trees and it's all magic. And this natural gas, or gas like it, doesn't start *any* wars, oh no.

It requires a bit of a mental shift to stop blaming poorer countries. Before, I found it easier to sit on a sprayed weird-green lawn (possibly sipping a mint julep) and give out about what lower-income countries were doing to their nature to provide cooking heat for their children. But you know, we'd got rid of a lot of our own nature already. And 180 years ago there was even less of it because there were more of us in Ireland. And you just know what the British – and definitely the Americans – said about us then: *they're having too many children.*

Plenty of timber gets cut down to fuel our lifestyle too. It's just that we don't do it personally and no one links us to it. But every cheap bit of flatpack furniture was a tree once, and, no, they're not all from sustainable forests. Plenty of reports link your too-cheap-to-be-true stool to illegal logging in Romania. So if you always find yourself in the kitchen at parties, maybe drop that one into the conversation.

We have two children. An heiress and an . . . er . . . heiress. We didn't stop at two because we are committed to taking care of the planet. The two, for all their adorability (we had them assessed by experts and it turns out they're THE BEST GIRLS ALTOGETHER), are enough. Maybe at the back of our minds we were aware that having a gaggle of them would give us the environmental impact of a small tannery works but, really, there were other non-environmental reasons, like we'd eventually have to move house. It's a standard corporation house, and I know your granny raised thirteen in it no problem and ye were happy, but your granny sent them all out onto the road to play and we can't do that because the SUVs are ignoring the 30 kph limit and using it as a rat run. And I work from home so three children in one room is the sort of nostalgia for the rare oul' times we decided we wouldn't embrace openly.

You don't need to know all this, but it's just to point out that the number of children in a family, whether it's zero or loads, is none of your business and it's unhelpful to make moral conclusions from it. It is the outcome of personal choice but also the context in which it takes place. So just stop it with the over-population thing.

It can't be denied, though: kids, they do consume the darndest things.

Bin there, done that

We were efficient. Our lives were optimized. I don't mean that we had done Lean Six Sigma courses in project management and were certified ninjas in leading stand-up meetings in developer scrums while aggressively driving down costs, all while maximizing customer KPIs. I just mean we had full control over our lives – what we bought, what we used and what we threw away. We could decide, on a whim, or having read something online, to try and Cut Back On X, because of, ya know, the whole sustainability thing. Mostly we were fairly milquetoast. This was in Sustainable 1.0, which was mainly just:

- don't personally cut down a rainforest but don't ask if one is being cut down on your behalf

- putting stuff in the green bin

It turned out I wasn't even doing the recycling right. At some point a few years ago, I casually glanced through a 'things you can't put in the recycling bin' list, all set to congratulate myself. 'What is the matter with people?' I said to myself. 'Why can't they recycle properly?' And then I read the article and realized I was 'people'. I'd been doing a thing known as wish-cycling, which was throwing stuff in and letting other people sort it out. Which is just genteel dumping. Plastic bags, bits of tinfoil, bits of plastic that could loosely be described as 'the yoke off the thing'. I also wasn't thinking of the people who had to sort it. I'm sure if I had met them and we got chatting at a wedding and they told me, 'You wouldn't believe the shit people throw in the green bin,' I would never have committed some of the green-bin crimes. But until then, they were out of sight, out of mind. There I was thinking I was as sustainable as Bear Grylls on an island with only some lice, his own piss and a production team to keep him warm.

The pre-kids kidding-ourselves included self-congratulation over how rarely the general waste bin went out. We were practically off-grid. It was only to be used for weirdos like a discarded door handle. And maybe once in a while some organic waste that we didn't have the stomach or the gas mask to deal with. The forgotten chicken breasts storing god knows what beneath their filmy covers – I wasn't going to be separating that into its constituent parts, opening the packet and unleashing a resident evil, like a melting permafrost giving anthrax a chance to express itself for the first time since it killed its last mammoth. But other than that, very little went to landfill. We were smug. 'See that black bin there?' we'd say at exclusive gatherings, gesturing out the window. 'Hasn't gone out in months' – without really thinking about how much of the green bin ended up in landfill because the load was ruined.

But when children arrived, Black-Bin Day became D-Day. Every single thing they had seemed disposable, starting with nappies and wipes. Piles upon piles of them arrived into the house in bouncy, smiling plastic packets, playfully drop-kicked into the Baby Stuff Box from where they were dragged seconds later to be used, sometimes in poo-mageddon situations. Other times whole multipacks were decimated by mischievous multi-pees, whereby they'd pee all the way through the changing process so it became some sort of differential equation to solve to find the exact moment they had a dry nappy on. After months of inaction, the black bin now *had* to go out each fortnight. Miss it too often and it was going to be 1970s industrial-action Winter of Discontent levels of waste around the place. The signature roar of the engine outside on exhausted mornings was a diesel-powered alarm, the child-addled brain working out which day it was. *Is it Tuesday? Which Tuesday is it? Black Tuesday or green–brown Tuesday? And which of the thirty-five post-privatization bin companies is it today?* Then I'd use the sound to try to gauge proximity and whether the engine roar was advancing or receding. *Have I time to run out with the bin? Is the bin already out?* And, finally, *Am I wearing clothes?* When the truck came, it seemed to strain while lifting our bin. Was I imagining it or was the front of the truck itself lifting slightly, like a video in one of those Men Driving Diggers Lol-Banter Facebook groups?

It offended us. All this waste from our two little squidges. We weren't going to hand them back or anything. There are laws. But I think it surprised us, this very visual impact of creating new human beings.

We changed – at least partially – to cloth nappies. Do you remember cloth nappies? They may seem a vestige of an older time. Black-and-white interviews with stoic women in front of ranges telling the priest from the documentary team how many children they had and just how rare the oul' times were in Dublin City. (Ireland had an entire stream of documentaries made by priests for decades, called *Radharc*. Despite being set up by Ireland's equivalent of an ayatollah, Archbishop John Charles McQuaid, they were often critically acclaimed.) I was raised in old black-and-white nappies. Possibly in them for too long. But I bet you suspected that.

Cloth nappies have changed a bit since my childhood. The terry nappies with the pastel-coloured safety pins that some-times opened were really just squares of cloth. They gave me the loin-clothed-holy-man-on-top-of-a pillar look. Over them went 'plastic pants' – a small-child's-bottom-shaped mattress protector. Now, the nappies are way swankier, with fleecy lining and Velcro, and the covers are all lovely bright colours with smiling teddy bears and unicorns. But a bit like those videos of photogenic North Korean children playing enormous guitars in unison, cute and colourful but masking a dark secret. Content warning: shit.

Washable nappies force you to come to terms with shit in a way that is far more fundamental than disposable ones do. When it's disposable, you can almost change them one handed – open the nappy, try and mask the initial horror on your face at the chaotic evil in front of you, so as to reassure the child you will still be there tomorrow, and then dramatically reach for wipes to staunch . . . everything.

But you get to fold it all away, wrap it up, bring it out to the Bad Bin and vow never to speak of it again, until the child gurgles 10 minutes later like a Shit-Columbo – *Oh, just one more thing . . .* But still, apart from disasters on the side of the road, or in polite company when you are wearing light-coloured trousers, it's containable.

Washable ones need to be washed. But before that they need to be tipped. You hope it's tippable – otherwise it's all going in the nappy bin, a receptacle that has to be stored outside like an upright septic tank. Then you haul the nappy sack out of the bin and in from the garden, forcing it into the washing machine, checking the door seal afterwards, like one of those worst medieval jobs ever in *Horrible Histories*.

There are a few points about all this Too Much Information. It makes you think about waste. We saved a few thousand nappies from landfill (some might have gone to incineration but 15 per cent of municipal waste went to landfill as of 2019). A disposable nappy takes about 250 years to decompose. I think less about the environmental damage of that because I still haven't got my head around thinking of landfill as 'the earth'. It's sort of a limbo. It's the dump, so what else would be there anyway? And all that plastic eventually comes back to us in our food supply, but we don't taste it. I think more about the fact that a load of child poo is being preserved for future archaeologists to discover and somehow trace it back to us and think, *They locked away their shit? Why? That stuff decomposes after a week.*

Cloth nappies saved a bit of money in the end. There's carbon footprint in washing them and growing the cotton, and we did release a chunk of washing powder into the sewage system. But still, by and large, there is no calculus that says reuse of a thing is worse than throwing it away. As I've said, your personal choices are good, yes, they help, but systematic change is what's needed. But this is one personal choice where you can see a big impact straight away. The Evil Bin needs to be emptied less. And, more importantly, it makes you think more about disposable-ness.

But, but, but . . . for washable nappies you need the following:

- A washing machine. Not everyone has one and no one's going to bring shite-bags to the launderette.

- Somewhere to hang them – a washing line outside. Baby-occupied homes are full enough as it is of babygros drying on radiators.

- Upfront money. They are cheaper in the long run but cloth nappies cost a bit more up front, even the second-hand ones we bought. You can try them out by borrowing them from a cloth-nappy library. No, 'nappy library' does not refer to an archive of poo, a time capsule for future coprologists. It's a community of other clothers (I made up that term) who loan you nappies to give it a try. Yet another reason why libraries of any kind are the last bastion of socialism hidden in plain sight.

- Time. Shit takes time. Time is money. Or in the case of having small children, time is a mystery.

- Someone willing to do it. Not wanting to tip poo into a toilet or examine the rubbery bit of a washing machine door is *not* a failure of character. Being motivated to do it is not a measurement of sainthood. It's a combination of the ease of availability of the previous four factors and then being up for it, a bit of positive reinforcement and seeing some results. And knowing other people who are doing it.

- Pragmatism. Consider bringing a few disposables for
  outings and visits. No one needs a stinky martyr in their
  lives.

On the other side of the coin, disposable nappies are amazing
technology. Whatever age you are, you just pee and it's gone.
They use sodium polyacrylate, aka a super-absorbent
polymer that can absorb a hundred to a thousand times its
mass in water – just like in the nappy ads where they pour
blue water during the science bit. I've picked up enough
one-ton rain-sodden ones discarded in ditches to appreciate
just how good they are. Now, if you google sodium polyacrylate you'll find all sorts of warnings from studies. But
there's no point in getting into studies in this book. There's
too much back and forth. *And anyway it was in mice.*

That's why I think cloth nappies are one good microcosm
for the dilemma we all experience about Making a Personal
Change in your life versus What's the Point? We can't sugar-
coat it. (Although disposable nappies have a coating on them
that according to studies could cause – no, forget it.) It's not
enough by itself: it needs to have a bit of reward, people
need to acknowledge it's hard, it shouldn't be a moral
crusade and you need a bit of community to keep you going.
And the default way of doing things is easy and cheaper
upfront and has the full weight of some of the largest companies in the world doing the sciencing and marketing. It
would help if the more time-consuming method of doing
things had official support.

It's not a straightforward choice between beautiful home-
spun squares of cloth woven on looms by a happy band of
Bennetton-ad diverse craftspeople and EVIL NAPPYTECH.

The cotton industry is polluting, exploitative, carbony. You have to do a bit of a life-cycle assessment because you can't just get away with 'feeling good'. We got around this by buying the nappies second-hand so we didn't add to the awfulness of their inception, and we sold them second-hand too.

One side effect of getting down and dirty is it forces us to deal with our own shite. Not just literal shite – anything at all that comes out of either our bodies or our houses. We have been on a centuries-long journey to avoid looking at, seeing, smelling or hearing waste. We have a huge fear of ick. It's understandable. Disgust for the ick that dominates our taboos and our swear words is millennia old, and it kept us alive as we started to settle in groups. We had to pipe it out, dispose of it. The Babylonians had a sewage network 6,000 years ago. But in sanitizing it away from our immediate vicinity, we have lost touch with the consequence of our own actions – be it the super-absorbent lining that keeps your baby's bottom nice and dry through the night, or our recycling whisked away to be dealt with by humans and machines we never see, or the online clothes we bought. But shite used to be gold. Guano, dung, even our piss was used too. Everyone had pigs. We all smelled, to varying degrees, of shite.

Only farmers and horticulturalists and ecologists remain dung aware, but as people realize just how much we rely on natural gas to make stuff grow without poo, you're going to hear a lot more about poo.

Picky

But if it isn't one end it's the other. They tend not to eat rare grains, these children. Oh, how we scoffed at parents we saw shovelling yellow food-units into their children in certain restaurants. *It's just breaded 'stuff'. Would you even call it chicken? Mmmm, these tomatoes are AMAZING. When we are parents our children will be eating only fresh ingredients. They will browse the shrubbery like little goats, getting all those as-yet-unspecified minerals into them like their ancestors. They will be noble and primal.*

We didn't know then that bready, spuddy, meaty, yellowy-whitey food is what children gravitate towards. There is a primeval urge. Deep within them is the fear they are going to be poisoned by berries and bracken so they go for the most colourless, bland food possible because it should be the least likely to injure them. Which drives them into the arms of Massive Big Yellow, which makes food slurry out of tankers of fishmeal, chicken protein and something that was once a grain grown on land that's 80 per cent Gramoxone. And then there is the fundamental urge to eat things with as much packaging as possible – endless plastic pouches with plasticky lids, and why wouldn't they eat the ones we make for them with the reusable pouches? And when you make something for them it seems almost impossible to make a small enough amount of food for a small child. We will only know they are full when they scream and hurl the remainder of the food across the room like a bored tyrant . . . And then you have to drive places we could *definitely* walk to, only their little legs get tired. And then the clothes . . . You try to get them second-hand as much as possible but they grow out of them so fast, and the *shoes* – don't get me started on the shoes! Everyone blowing smoke up Ernest Hemingway's hole about his six-word story, 'For sale: baby shoes, never worn', and it was just about how he got a load of presents when the youngest was born and never even *saw* these shoes until it was too late and they were too small. What a waste. And then the children grow up and probably want fast fashion and devices made out of conflict rare earths and drink €10 hot chocolate before breakfast in a disposable cup that they'll just throw on the ground because I saw teenagers do that once on a programme, and they'll forget all about the environment until it is destroyed completely and then they'll be in the wasteland looking at me, saying, 'Why did you bring us into this?' and, and, and . . .

This is the kind of thought process that I sometimes slip into, a cascade of 'and then something worse will happen's. And to snap myself out of it, I think about why having children is a good thing for the environment, sometimes.

First of all, at the most petty level, children do put a stop to your gallop, soften your cough, take the wind out of your sails, put diesel in your petrol tank. I know measuring your carbon footprint in terms of spur-of-the-moment weekend breaks to European cities is a grey area. But I can definitely say we have helped in our own tiny way to reduce demand for €4 flights to Prague by not going abroad as often in the last seven years.

Also, I consume less stuff. The massive move of emotional weight from caring about myself to caring for two other people seems to have had an impact in how many things I get for myself. It's not being noble. It just seems to be about settling into a comfortable level of dadliness, where stuff for me is less important. I repeat, this is not because of goodness. They've just sapped me of self-care capabilities. I haven't looked at the science, but I'm fairly sure that children emit some sort of chemical that mesmerizes you into believing old tracksuit bottoms and washed-out T-shirts are all you need. Maybe it's the oxytocin. It's to stop me going out gallivanting or buying things. Anyway, there's no point having nice things around the house because they'll only wreck them with Petit Filous.

Now let me be quite clear, lest that paragraph be screenshot out of context, I DO NOT mean that having children necessarily makes you less selfish and that if you don't have them you are selfish. I mean that in *my* case, me and my wife were mainly focused on each other. Others may be completely devoted to doing good for society and the arrival of children would actually interrupt that work. As ever, the legal disclaimer applies: 'Description of one's own experience is not to be taken as direct criticism of someone else's experience.'

So, so far, maybe the two children are carbon neutral. (Citation needed. [Checked: there is no citation.]) But eventually they'll grow up and we'll outgrow the cuddles. They'll want to visit their friends who live in a place not served by public transport, they'll have hobbies that require megawatts of energy, and the four of us will start polluting and consuming as autonomous people again. While they're going on ski holidays to human-rights-disregarding desert states, I'll be drinking gold-flake Bellinis at London Fashion Week as I scout the latest trends in lads sauntering down the catwalk dressed in asbestos and palladium. We'll wear scarves indoors and spend thousands on disposable sieves because I just *can't* deal with washing them any more.

It depends on what careers they have, though. They may go to work as yacht designers for oligarchs, as PR people for large oil companies, as customer-joy specialists for a company that makes bot farms to flood the comments of farming groups' Facebook pages with points about how climate-change propaganda is the work of the Illuminati, and people should really check out Russell Brand's latest video where he spills the tea on What They Don't Want You to Know.

But there's a chance they might work on bacteria that eat plastic or wind turbines that don't kill birds, or find a way to ensure that farmers are paid more for food so they can create more space for nature while also ensuring the poor are not priced out. Or grow food themselves. Or be electricians specializing in fixing solar panels. Or be water engineers to reduce toilet poverty. Or work in social justice, because environmental improvements without equality for people who are worse off are not worth a shite.

Maybe my two will square a thousand circles. Or maybe they won't. They don't have to do anything beyond the normal things we all do to stay reasonably physically and mentally healthy, feel secure, have some basic expectation of getting to do things that they get a kick out of, be surrounded or accompanied by people who like and love them, and have or not have children. (But they really should because I would love to have a go at being a grandparent.)

That's all they could do and their presence would still be good for the environment.

Because the presence of children, regardless of how many there are in each family, is optimism writ large. Whether they're your children, relatives, neighbours, even the ones in the ads, they're a reason to keep trying to do the right thing to ensure they've a fighting chance at living in a live-able world.

And I don't mean in the sense that you hope their taxes will pay for your adult nappies and insulin and a million and one other things we'll need when we're older that we mightn't have the physical ability to earn ourselves. I know we joke about having children mainly to have someone to mind us. (Some langers even use it as a stick to beat people who don't have children. *Oh, that's all very well for you to say with your spur-of-the-moment decisions and lie-ins and Insta-ing your cinnamon rolls while we stand on the side of a freezing pitch. Well, our children are going to be* . . . Take a step back. Who knows where we'll all be? People who are childfree now might end up minding you because they've managed to conserve energy while you were up all night worrying about Leaving Cert points and whether you'd said the wrong thing to another parent in the playground.)

But looking after children means equipping them to deal with an uncertain future. In our blessed period of peace between World Wars II and III, that previously meant the basic stuff of how to behave in groups, how to think for yourself, how to make friends, how to make enough money to give you a decent chance at fleeting moments of happi-ness, how to treat other people, how to treat other people if they're a complete pain in the hole, how to not lie awake at night worrying if you're the pain in the hole. But to that we now need to add how to deal with a changing climate and very damaged nature.

It has to start with trying to explain what the fuck is going on without depressing the hell out of them. A certain school of thought suggests we are burdening children by telling them. But I don't know if you've ever been subjected to questioning by children. They grind you down. Their memories are prodigious. They remember all your previous bullshit rules so when you attempt to wriggle out of an answer they will 'But, Daddy, remember before you said . . .' you faster than Matlock reducing the cocky witness to guilt-admitting tears.

I was burdened with bad news growing up. There was nothing else on the telly. We had to whisht for the news and you best believe I heard it all. And no one was dashing up to turn off something distressing. We didn't have a remote control until 1987, and prior to that we had to change the channel with the knob from the paraffin heater – the fabled Paraglo. A heater that made you acutely aware of the impact of fossil fuels by pumping the fumes from burning kerosene right into your cakehole so the place smelled like a refinery city. Some heat out of it, though, in fairness, as literally nothing was lost to transmission.

So I saw a lot of bad news: Lebanon, South American dictators, Chernobyl, acid rain, Iran–Iraq war, the Troubles in the North. I wrote a poem in 1988 called 'My Hopes for '88' which had the line 'I hope the soldiers in the Gaza Strip/

will pack up their belongings and take a trip'. We worried about nuclear radiation and the Devil.

And I'm fine. I think. I mean, I like a drink of a Monday lunchtime BUT WHO DOESN'T?

I don't believe children need to be protected from the bad news in the world. The challenge is to get the balance right without provoking nightmares (like the ones I had about Druze militia chasing me around the fields).

They ask me about picking up rubbish. Picking up rubbish is an easy one to analogize because I'M SICK AND TIRED OF PICKING UP THEIR TOYS AROUN – sorry, I mean they understand litter and that it's bad. They understand using every bit of scrap paper to draw on – not because there's a shortage but because it's bad to throw things away that haven't been used a few times. They know some toys are second-hand – apart from the ones Santa brings which were definitely not bought from a fella in Finglas one night in early November. I don't get into the details of microplastics being found in placentas or a turtle with a disposable mask (STAY SAFE, EVERYONE) wrapped around its neck. I need them to know and be aware without being damaged.

I try and map waste to a bigger thing. Switching off unneeded lights (at which I am now a champion) is not to reduce the electricity bill (WAIT, OF COURSE IT IS) but mainly to get them thinking about how energy is everything and it comes from somewhere, and everything we do requires something to be taken from the environment, and there's no need to have a light on if there's no one in the room, and CLOSE THAT DOOR – WE'RE NOT HEATING THE ROAD.

I need to be honest with them but not brutally honest. They're already learning that humans are complicated, that Mammy and Daddy spend a lot of time trying to figure out how to tell another adult something in a way that doesn't come across as 'I dunno, a bit . . . like . . . you know' instead of just telling them. That there are disappointments and setbacks. That we make mistakes and get it wrong but try to keep going and not be cynical. I won't tell them about Daddy's raging hypocrisy straight away. They'll need to have *some* faith in authority to get them past under-7s in the GAA. And they'll need to have the absolute idealism and sense of purpose that small children excel at, the kind of drive that makes a child say, 'I'm going to make a space city out of the cardboard box the Paraglo came in,' and for it to look nothing like it – not even close – but it doesn't bother them.

But what I want them to feel is that, when it comes to being part of any work to help the planet, I'm happy to help them in any way I can. And if we get it wrong, we'll start again. The biggest favour I can do for them is to not be cynical and to help them avoid it too.

The discount store

The final thought about the next generations is a weird abstract one that I haven't fully grasped the impact of yet. And it's not even about my children. It's about my grandchildren or someone else's. Anyone not born yet. It doesn't take a genius to know that billions of children will be born over the next thirty years. Some of them I will love and hopefully dandle on my knee as pudgy-faced toddlers and play with and then, if they start crying or do an enormous poo, hand back to their parents. These children do not exist in the physical sense, but we know they will at some point. Maybe I'll never meet them. But I will have a small impact on them.

It's about a thing called discounting. When we think of future people, they're sort of fuzzy. They're not protesting or giving out to us. They've no votes. They can't make us feel guilty. I hadn't thought about them until I started reading about the concept of intergenerational justice. Now, says you, I've enough to be worrying about being nice to people around me without worrying about future people. But we already care *a bit* for people we'll never meet. We pay taxes. We give to charity. We run up Kilimanjaro on a sponsored something.

The people in the future are no more distant, just less specific. But they're treated officially differently. Their lives are officially not worth as much. Because of the discount rate. Discounting.

It works roughly along the following lines. Spending €100 on a present benefit to an existing voting, complaining human is worth more than spending €100 on a longer term project that will likely benefit a future human. Like, say, fixing climate change. The extent to which spending the 100 euro on me is worth more than spending it on my imagined grandchildren depends on the discount rate.

Governments have to decide what the rate is when figuring out whether to fund something long term. So they discount the value to future generations of a thing, which effectively discounts the future people's value as humans. If the discount rate is 2%, it means (kind of like the reverse of a compound interest formula) that spending 100 euro for a future thing gives us 37 euro of benefit now. Basically the future human is not worth as much as the present one. I've simplified the shite out of that. There's inflation, opportunity cost, uncertainty (an asteroid might kill us all anyway). But it also comes back to the basic, most human of things. A biscuit now is worth more to us than a promise of a future biscuit.

And ordinarily I might have been thinking, *Too right, fuck 'em.* But since I became directly responsible for two people, my concept of the future has changed. I know it should have been part of me anyway, part of a commitment to those far into the future, like it is for a number of peoples around the world. For example the Haudenosaunee of North America, who believe that decisions we make today should be made with those seven generations hence in mind. I was just a standard short-term bollox. But since having children, the concept of their future lives and what I do to influence that has actually changed. We already do it on the money side. We might save for their education or keep an eye on the dysfunctional housing situation here and think, *what sacrifice can I make now to make sure they've a place to live in future, even if I know they won't be grateful enough?*

But what about their air or water quality? They don't become water purifiers at the age of eighteen. Like, I'm already spending a load of money on their current welfare – wouldn't it make sense to spend it on their adult wellbeing too? And that of their children or niblings? I hadn't thought like this before. It doesn't dominate my thoughts all the time, but like a lot of things, now I can't unknow it. I tell ya, it's hard enough worrying about your own children without thinking about possible ones.

8.

Oh stop, don't be talking to me

*'Look, I don't know what other way to
explain it to ya. It just stopped working'*

**– gas man trying to explain to me
why a valve had stopped working**

I'd love to be handy. To walk into a situation all Snickers-trousered and authoritative, turn to the house-owner and say with a sigh, 'Who put that in for you?' Having trades-people in the house is generally a procession of them asking why the previous job was done that way and what the fuck were they at at all, and me not knowing and mumbling that they must have had their reasons. Then the tradesperson does the job and explains to me what's going on, and I nod and listen and ask questions and promptly forget the answer. It doesn't happen at the doctor's, usually. They don't tell you to pull down your trousers then point at your bits and say, 'Who put that in for ya, in the name of god? Was it one of our lads? Was he registered?'

There has been a decline in handiness as the generations have gone by. Or certainly in my case. Dada could do most things. I'm not saying he could do them to the level of a master craftsperson, but he got them done. He'd give anything involving car fixing, bits of wiring, small building jobs, water, some appliances a go. Just handy jobeens.

It comes with the territory of farming. Maintenance is just a relentless hum. Wind, rain, vegetation, animals and Time are 'never not at it'. There isn't the leeway to be waiting for A Man to come and fix things. You go out with the yoke and fix the other yoke.

Farming is different now in that not everything is a directly observable lever or wire. There's a lot more software. I presume if the calving monitor attached to the cow's tail shows an error has occurred because of a paper jam in area C, an expert will need to be called.

Eventually Dada got a bit shook and had less of the confidence to just go out and do it. More specialists came to the house. And as time went on, those experts started to be hearing, mobility, health experts, and we knew that his days of general tipping away in the workshop with something to do with the vice-grips were gone forever. And he wasn't going to be acquiring any new skills apart from bits of physio and different types of tablets. He never got a handle on mobile phones, mainly because they didn't have a handle on them. Indeed, any kind of screen where the link between a mechanical operation and a result has been broken annoyed him. He liked switches, levers, pulleys, knobs that turned. Fiddly yokes were the bane of his life.

I don't have the Snickers-workwear confidence (although I wouldn't rule out buying a pair – the pockets!) and like many a child of a handy parent, I suffer by comparison. Obviously I'm the one doing all the comparing. No one else cares. It's not to say I don't have skills. They're just not exactly whittling. I'm better at motorway exits, for example. Depending on your age, turning left off a road in order to go right will never not be weird. I also have a very good sense when scrolling for highlights of a goal on Twitter whether rights are available in my area or not. They just don't teach that kind of thing in school. I can find properties seized by the Criminal Assets Bureau on Google Street View because of the size of the gates and the swimming pool taking up the entire back yard. But it's not as satisfying or marketable as going at a thing with a sledge hammer (which funnily enough is what attracted the attention of the Criminal Assets Bureau to the house in the first place).

The lack of handiness makes it a bit annoying when trades-people explain what they're doing. Hence the long conversation with the gas man a few months ago. (Natural gas, not naturally funny.) He was trying to explain the thermostatic valve had stopped working due to pressure drops because something, something, mains supply. I was struggling. He'd explain something, then I'd try to repeat it to show I understood. But it soon became apparent that what was in his head was not going to fit in my head, no matter how much he simplified it for me.

But despite this desire to know, I take many things completely on faith and make no effort to actually understand how they work. And, mainly, that's fine. When you get in a plane you don't think about Bernoulli's principle, which links density and velocity to the pressure variations of moving air that allows lift. You just want people to step in from the aisle when they're stowing their luggage, and as the 500-tonne plane leaves the ground and your bottom slightly leaves your body, you just browse the box sets.

When you take paracetamol you don't think about how it acts in two separate ways, both through the inhibition of cyclooxygenase and the actions of its metabolite, AM404. You just trust that it 'eases pain' and maybe think about an ad where a cartoon head gets less red around the brain bit. You accept that other people have done the work, it's cheap, it seems to work and – is that the time?

More recently, I did some research into my qualifications and it turned out I wasn't a virologist. And there wasn't enough time to skill up on how a virus spike protein binds to the ACE2 receptor on the host cell or to observe it happening, so I had to take certain things on faith. I believed the scientists when they said this coronavirus was a bad thing that goes from person to person through the air and surfaces, so while they were figuring out what the hell was going on, less people sharing air and surfaces might be a good idea, as would wiping the ones you can't avoid. I believed that since snot and water vapour come out of your mouth and nose some sort of mask – a decent one worn properly on your face, not your ear – would be of help. And since a lot of scientists and 200 years of vaccine history are broadly positive, I'd probably trust a vaccine as a thing that's safer to take than not take.

Why was I happy to clearly drink the Big Pharma Kool Aid? To participate in the Great Reset? To be a willing fool for the New World Order? Was it that I was happy to sleep-walk into the enslavement of the people to turn them into mindless drones for Big Tech so that Big Tech can . . . er . . . um . . . well, I still haven't figured out that bit.

So my need to feel handy and ask questions of the gas man means, yes, I'd love to be an expert on climate models, but I am going to satisfy myself with the following basic rules of believing a thing.

Does it make sense?

Does the big thing I'm being asked to believe roughly make sense to me, an idiot? I've basically believed climate change for ages without understanding what was going on, so I read a book about the science of climate change and now I know enough to roughly understand it. I'll tell you if you like. If you're having doubts. Or if you find yourself easily derailed – as I did – by someone.

So, are temperatures going up? Yes. That's sure as sure can be. At the South Pole, snow from a million years ago is somewhere deep in the ice. If you drill down and take out a slice, you can get that snow and also the air trapped in it. It's a screenshot. From the oxygen in that snow slice they can work out the temperature. Looking at the temperature across hundreds of thousands of years, they know it's warmer and getting warmer faster than ever before. Okay, that I can grab. I don't know the chemistry but that *feels* right. It falls into paracetamol territory.

Then is there more CO_2? Yes. The same slices of ice or soil at the bottom of a lake or rings of trees all tell us there's more CO_2 than ever before. And it's going up faster than ever before. It used to go up and down, up and down, up and down, gently with ice ages and sun cycles and whatnot. Now it's going UP, UP, UP, UP, UP.

Did we do that? Yes. The UP, UP, UP, UP, UP started after the Industrial Revolution. Also, we can measure the amount of coal, oil and gas we burned because we know how much was mined or drilled, we know how much is stored, and take one number from the other and that's the burnt stuff.

Does CO_2 make the place warmer? Yes. This is the hardest bit to understand, so first you have to smoke something strong, look at your hands, get existential and just appreciate what a miracle the Earth is. I don't mean that it is a beautiful jewel and you throwing away your chip bag is destroying it. I mean think about how perfect the temperature is most of the time, so most of its surface is liveable. But if you go into space you'll freeze. Even if you head *towards the sun*. So there's something around the Earth that makes it liveable. The atmosphere.

The atmosphere is the insulation that allows the sun to heat us up – from the energy from sunlight – and for all that heat energy not to bounce back into space in the form of infra-red. Like a greenhouse, it lets the sunlight in and doesn't let as much heat out.

The atmosphere is not glass. It's a mixture of gases. And the precise mixture of gases keeps in a certain amount of heat. One of the gases in the atmosphere is CO_2. And the amount of CO_2 is more than before.

So what? That proves nothing. There are more Bluetooth connections in the atmosphere than before too, but no one's saying that listening to podcasts while cycling is causing climate change (actually, we release about 12 kilos each a year of carbon listening to podcasts but, sure, it keeps us off the streets).

The thing about carbon dioxide is it's a greenhouse gas, which means it allows heat energy from the sun to pass through it, but when that heat is reflected back out from the surface of the earth towards space, CO_2 and other greenhouse gases trap it and force it back down to us. It's like a valve that only goes one way or a bullock that has no problem finding its way into someone's lawn but can't for the life of it find the gap on the way back out.

We need greenhouse gases to make the place liveable, otherwise we'd be frozen. There are three main ones: carbon dioxide from plants and burning stuff, methane from some bogs and animal belches and a bit of industry, and nitrous oxide from industry, engines and agriculture.

All of those things increased in recent centuries. There are more greenhouse gases. More heat gets trapped. Therefore the planet is warming up mostly because of stuff we did. That's something I can get my head around. If I wanted, I could try and explore electromagnetic radiation as it passes a CO_2 molecule, how the bonds between the C and the two Os are like springs, creating a wavelength range that gets absorbed, something about dipoles and nanometres – but I would be spoofing. I have enough to conceptualise this difficult planet-wide problem into something small and manageable. If I try to explain it further to someone in a pub, I know I'll forget bits and lose track and appear uncon-vincing and as if I'm hiding something. But I now know enough to spend no more time getting derailed by someone who doesn't believe in it. I'll tell them what I know and then they can go away. That is purely to save time. Because the main thing we definitely know is we don't have time for retreading the argument.

Who else believes it?

The next step in believing something is to ask who else believes it. And the answer in this case is nearly everyone. Apparently 97 per cent of scientists agree climate change is real and it's caused by us. I got that number from the NASA website. Can NASA be trusted? I mean, like, they did fake the moon landings and all the movies about the moon landings so who knows what they can do? But I struggle to see a motivation for them reporting this because climate change is bad for their business, given they burn a hell of a lot of rocket fuel just to get to space.

Isn't 97 per cent a bit too high? You only see 97 per cent when a government issues a report on its own progress and, it turns out, they're doing amazingly! Or in an election, when the stripe-shouldered brigadier who swore he would return the country to democracy is still, thirty years and four houses on the Côte D'Azur later, knocking it out of the park in the voting results – 97 per cent, in fact, and over 100 per cent in some areas.

So 97 per cent agreement on a matter as complicated as how a 6-billion-trillion-ton planet interacts with its 6-quadrillion-ton atmosphere, 8 billion people, 20 quintillion animals, 410 quintillion joules of solar energy received, 120,000 terawatts of fossil-fuel energy burned every year and a squillion other variables? Well, that's quite an agreement. And the fact that climate models as far back as 1970 predicted reasonably accurately where we are today, even though they were using abacuses and crayons back then? It's very hard to get that right through hard work. Even harder to fake it.

But, but, but what about groupthink? Didn't everyone believe one time that the world was flat and you could cure things with leeches? No one with a brain ever thought the world was flat – not for the last 2,500 years. In fact, the first time I heard about it was when we learned about Christopher Columbus in school and that some sailors were afraid to go on the ship with him because they thought they'd fall off the edge of the world. But this was made up in the nineteenth century in a book about him by Washington Irving (the 'Rip Van Winkle' guy).

It doesn't mean science doesn't get things wrong. It just means that we'd probably know by now if it was spectacularly off. So suspiciously dictator-votely high as that 97 per cent is, they're probably right.

But what if all of these scientist types, these greens, these humourless doomsayers, are only in it for the money? Those sweet research grants. Or maybe they have shares in 'Green Companies' that make 'Green Stuff'.

This is entirely possible. You *might* spend ages pretending to pore over the details of a thousand climate models each containing WAAAAHOObytes of information just to confirm the temperature is going up or the Amazon has turned from a carbon sink into a carbon . . . not-sink. Maybe you're in league with Elon Musk and you'll just send the armies after the lithium instead of the oil.

But I just think we'd *know* by now if there was a coverup. We found out about the coverup by the oil companies in the late seventies who knew burning fossil fuels caused climate change and said, 'Oh, shit, this can't get out.'

I'm going to go out on a limb and suggest that no one on the green side has that much invested to make making stuff up incredibly lucrative. Apart from a few Andrew Wakefield types, it seems like a terrible way to make money. There must be easier ways.

What if they're all wrong?

So, what if they've got it wrong? What if it's just the sun being weird? Well, for a start, it's really unlikely, but let's say that they were wrong. Personally I'd rather risk betting on Trying to Kill Less Nature and Digging Less Things up and Moving Them Around the World Just to Burn Them, and Maybe the Superrich Have Enough so Wouldn't It Be Nice to Try and Share Wealth a Bit More Fairly.

If the reasons for doing all of that turned out to be wrong and temperatures plummeted, then a lot of good would have been done. And if you needed oil and coal then, you could dig out it then. It won't go off. So if I had to be wrong, I'd rather be wrong that way.

On debating

But most people believe in climate change, don't they? Nearly all Irish people believe it's real. A majority of people around the world do. So why the need to prove it to myself if I'm happy enough to believe in it too? Well, first of all, there are still plenty of people who throw around oul' shite like 'I remember a warm summer in '53' or 'What about the snow in 2010?' Or 'Them scientists are always getting it wrong – remember Chernobyl?' Or ''Tis all a money-making racket'. And I use the same formula to try and negotiate what I feel about other things.

- Does it make rough sense?

- Are the people proposing it reasonable? Are they acting in good faith? Even if it turned out they were massively deluded, is the place they're coming from rooted in a broadly positive purpose?

- If it was wrong, would doing something about it be a bad thing?

Some decisions are easy – they just make sense. Cycling is easy. If I can cycle between two destinations *and back*, then literally the only emissions are farts. The car will burn something. And I'll still fart but they'll be stress ones. That's so easy. So it stands to reason that the system helping me and a few hundred thousand others make that decision easier is just going to be better.

If I drive slower I'll burn less fuel. Easy. The only variable is time. But no one needs 20 minutes that much. It's an Avensis, not an ambulance. Again, if the Government says 'drive slower', it's an easy win.

If it's harder for the heat to escape out of the building, I'll need to import less energy into the house to stay warm. So let's insulate the houses while waiting for the heat-pump fella to get back to us with a quote.

If less food is wasted, we don't need to buy as much to feed ourselves.

If we make and buy less stuff then we'll use less energy and stuff to make it. It's a simple equation. Some stuff you need, some stuff you don't. Separate out the stuff that we don't need and decide if we can make less of it. There's no real argument against that. I mean, unless you argue that we should make stuff purely for the purpose of generating income to pay for other people to fix climate change – and that sounds like emptying the hoover onto the floor just to get to use the hoover.

But for other questions about how we eat, travel, stay warm, have fun, raise a family, vote, buy, consume, there are going to be huge debates left right and centre with lots of valid points about inequality and whatnot. And it can be hard for the eejit like me to track and know what to believe. I don't mean that I sit in my favourite chair in my favourite dad-trousers with tea and biscuits and say, 'Ah, there's good and bad in all people. You know, Mussolini was a fierce man for the trains, in fairness to him.' I mean that the amount of information being launched back and forth can be bewildering. Debates are tiring. The emphasis is on winning rather than coming out of it knowing a bit more. And I used to do debating in school. Life was so much simpler then.

A lot of the debates were organized by Concern. The passage of time has distorted my memory, but all I remember debating was whether the IMF and World Bank fucked everything up for the Third World or they did it themselves. We had a teacher who passionately believed the former, so for many evenings after school I read pages and pages photocopied from books about how any number of countries in the developing world had been doing fine – or at least doing their own thing, feeding their people, paying their teachers and nurses, that sort of innocence. They didn't have SodaStreams or hydroelectric power but they were sort of tipping away. They needed a few bob extra to create jobs, though. And then the IMF or the World Bank or Top Banana or ChocolateMonsterCorp or some general amalgam of Absolute Bastards would come along, knock all the forests, take all the bauxite, poisoning the fish and leaving the place in shite.

If you had to argue the other side and say that, actually, ChocolateMonsterCorp were sound and a great crowd to pick cocoa for, you'd blame the dictator who wanted to build a 300-foot golden statue of his own ear lobe and needed money to pay for it. And over-population as well. That would turn up. What are they at in them countries with all the babies?

It seems that debate is focused on defeating the other argument, and if you accept the other side might have a point you are OWNED. Absolutely BODIED by the other side. I don't think we have time for that shit. I'd just like to know more. But how do you know what you *should* know? Who do you know that can tell you what to know about what to know?

I don't really know for definite. But to stop myself going mad, I have a process that I apply to 'debates' that seem complicated.

It's not that simple

First, I assume straight away that *it's probably more complicated than I think it is*. Because the last few years has taught me that, apart from –

'WHY ARE YOU LEAVING THE FUCKING ENGINE RUNNING IN YOUR CAR WHILE WAITING FOR SOMEONE? FOR FUCK'S SAKE. WHAT IS WRONG WITH YOU? THE TEMPERATURE OUTSIDE IS 14 DEGREES. YOU'RE IN ATHLONE, NOT ALBUQUERQUE. Sorry, I just . . . I promised I wouldn't condemn people, so I'm sure you have your reasons – actually, fuck that. What are you leaving the engine running for? That hasn't been necessary for about a decade of cars, old or new. You won't wear out the ignition. How expensive does diesel have to get for you to not burn it? Unless I have proof you're driving a 1987 Mirafiori that needs someone to open the bonnet to press down the choke, I think you can switch off the fucking engine, you absolute spoon . . . Oh, sorry, it's refrigerated to keep that transplanted organ alive?

Sorry for banging on your window. No, you carry on, Doctor, saving lives.

Yeah, most things need a bit of extra detail, so I've started assuming that complexity. Take plastic packaging on food. Someone has by now sent you a photo of a single banana wrapped in plastic with an eye-roll emoji. 'Ehm, excuse me, bananas already have packaging. It's called the *skin*.' Classic banter. High fives all around. But plastic around food reduces food waste. 'Ah, shite. I hate plastic. You're telling me it does some good? Feck.' But if you look further you might see that, in some cases, plastic packaging around fruit and veg actually increases food waste because the way it's packaged often makes you buy more than you need. So the guilt for throwing stuff out has been transferred to you. And we consumers do guilt much better than companies because we don't have a PR department to make us feel better. We just throw the shrivelled fruit and disappointed broccoli into the bin and eat a Purple Snack. Composting can only make you feel so good. It's the fifth of the five Rs. (But what I would say is that Ireland is almost always the leader in Europe for the amount of plastic packaging waste produced per head of population. I am not a plastics expert, and maybe as an island we need more things shipped in from longer distances, maybe as a food producer we send more stuff abroad wrapped in plastic, but it would be nice *not* to be the worst in Europe. Could we have that as a target?)

Or wind farms. They're good obviously. They'll kill a few birds but, you know, once you get them going . . . I'm sure the birds would be glad of the cleaner air. But what's this? Wind farms in bogs? Shure where else would you put them? But when you dig out the base and road to make the wind farm, you're making drains that drain the peat and leak out the carbon dioxide trapped in it like juice out of the Bolognese.

It's so fucking annoying that these things are so complicated. I was hoping to have this sorted by Tuesday week before I go on holidays. But I have to put the work into accepting extra complexity. That patience is as much a part of the job of being more environmentally conscious as planting a tree and tweeting about it. Because there are going to be more disappointments and setbacks and more nuance and complexity every time we try to do the right thing or just tackle any unforeseen consequence of modern life. So that'll be something to look forward to. But in the long run it saves time to understand complexity and as a result have a slower, more measured solution.

Assholes Part 2

Some people do assholey things; some people are just complete assholes. The dogshit-in-a-bag-tied-to-a-tree brigade (I mean the dogshit bag is tied to a tree, not the people who do it – although I would be okay with that form of punishment), I see them as being momentary assholes. I can't say for definite they are complete assholes. If you aggressively drive at cyclists: asshole. I don't see another way around it. You do it too often. You need to get some sort of help. And I guarantee you'll do it to someone else on the road. But people leaving the engine running – habit and forgetfulness for the most part. I've asked a few to stop and they have. They really didn't realize they were doing it.

I asked another fella and he told me to fuck off. He's an asshole.

People who throw rubbish out of a car window over a ditch in a rural area or general rural dumping: COMPLETE ASSHOLES. If you need to dump it, put it somewhere we can get it out of easy enough. Not into a fucking drain or into briars where the bag will rip and a baby hedgehog will drown in the rest of your Monster Energy drink, you prick. WORK WITH US HERE. BRING IT TO MY HOUSE AND I'LL PUT THE FUCKING THING IN MY BIN, ASSHOLE. It takes effort and diesel to do this. You're an asshole.

But all of these are still only civilian assholes. They are 'unarmed'. You could argue that it's a lack of education: they don't see it as wrong. It's habit. They are only a visible, active version of the assholey things we all do as consumers every time we buy a phone with blood-minerals in it or palm oil that decimated a mangrove swamp, take the car on a journey that could have been a walk or buy meat that came from a mistreated animal, because we don't have the time, inclination, money or knowhow or we can't be arsed to do it the less damaging way.

Not being arsed is the most human of things. We need a reason, a cause, an incentive, a bit of praise, a sense of community, a good feeling about ourselves as motivation for doing the right thing.

All this talk of assholery begs the inevitable question: am I an asshole? I haven't seen it in any of the self-help books at WHSmith in the airport, but I do think that, as well as manifesting and meditating and saying positive affirmations, we should, for self-care, just check in with ourselves to see if we're assholes. I'm definitely a hypocrite and incon-sistent and weak, and on a number of occasions I have been an asshole in the car or on a bike – just in rows – but if I average out the incidents, I'm self-grading as General-Population-Level Asshole. And I'm self-aware, which means I can try and do something about it, bit by bit. Starting next month. Or definitely the one after.

My gut feeling is that pure assholes are rare, and the biggest assholes are those who waste our time with arguments just for the sake of it. Cynics playing games. Delaying.

I have become less cynical over past few years – or at least I'd rather be wrong than assume the worst. It's the children. You don't have to have them to get this. Just be around them. Teachers, coaches, volunteers – they'll all say the same thing. Small children will wreck your head but their lack of cynicism is refreshing. Unless bad people have hurt them, most children believe people will try to do the right thing. Why wouldn't they? Why shouldn't we? At least to start with, anyway.

If I assume most people aren't assholes, then it's easier to take the next step and ask why they do what they do. I think most of our actions are for the same reasons: love, compan-ionship, being liked, being part of a group, security, money, a laugh, to make sure our families are safe.

Let's start with me. I make money out of this. I am being paid a few bob to write this book. There are more lucrative ways to make a living but ... like, I wouldn't *mind* if somehow this book sold a shitload of copies and I became the face for Hand-Wringing and Soul-Searching Without Doing a Whole Lot. It would be nice to be fêted all over the world and have ambassadors congratulate me and syco-phantic audiences throw softball questions at me like 'How did you do all of this while still looking so ripped?'

I have got the odd bit of work purely because I'm 'into this type of thing', but I get most of my work as an MC or come-dian because they hope I'll make people laugh. By and large, in the entertainment industry, corporate or club, they don't really give a shite about whether you plant the odd tree or pick up a bit of rubbish.

So I swear I'm not writing this book for the money. It's not worth it. I genuinely am just interested. But that doesn't mean I'm not compromised. My whole job depends on people having enough profits to pay for entertainment, so I'm not going to be opening up an industry awards ceremony by speaking absolute truth to power, ripping into the capi-talist system and telling all the participants the very fact they are 'growing their business' is killing the planet.

I write a monthly column for a farmers' paper. I like the job. I'd get by without it, but it definitely would stop me ripping into other writers for that paper if I disagreed with them.

Now, I don't intend to spend the money on helicopters or lots of stuff. Just the bills, savings for old age and being able to support my children when they enter Ireland's Worst Ever Accommodation Crisis in twenty years' time. I'd like to buy time with it and do a bit of nature restoration, like planting trees, or help spread good information. But I'm not pure. Maybe one day I'll be better. I also like to be liked. I don't like rows and will start blushing if challenged. If I'm as serious as I say I am, I'll have to grow a pair at some stage and take a chance on being more hard-core, more activisty, more able to deal with being targeted.

But I'm also very lucky. Because of the work I do, I'm not completely tied to one industry. I've no machinery or large work-based debt. My skills, such as they are, are reasonably transferrable.

So when it comes to the arguments, what are people's motivations? If your livelihood depends on doing things a certain way, climate change/nature crisis or not, it's hard to change tack. You see other industries that are not being existentially challenged. A swish tech company can have all the beehives they want on the roof of the office, but they're not being asked to stop using computers and leave half the office to rewild itself. So in classic Ted-Talk style, *my question to you is* 'What's your motivation?'

I don't know which side to pick

People we like often disagree with each other, and this makes it really hard for the casual observer trying to inform themselves about the environment. Sometimes I feel like a child whose parents are arguing and I want to shout, 'PLEASE STOP FIGHTING!' I like people who think that sheep are an abomination, an invasive species from Mesopotamia that have caused more damage to Ireland than Cromwell, and I also like people who have gorgeous flocks of sheep and gambolling lambs in beautiful meadows beneath ancient oaks. Are they both right or both wrong? Or is it just different sheep in different places? I like people who sell home heating oil and people who have huge expertise in renewable energy. I like vegans who grow their own protein and have the carbon foodprint of a sparrow, and I like big-jowled bon viveurs who post frankly pornographic pictures of steaks being ridden by Portobello mushrooms on social media.

I'd like to hope that a future Ireland where we are carbon neutral has room for all types of lifestyles, only 'a bit less so', if you know what I mean? So, my instinct is to meet conflict halfway and see what common ground there is.

But then again, maybe the wishy-washy middle grounder will be first up against the wall during the apocalypse. Committed people are needed for the After Times.

Going logo

So much of the discussion around what we can do to help the environment is fact-based and reasoned and calm. Some of it is passionate. But sometimes it sounds plausible and feels wrong. If you get the feeling that there's something not quite right about a debate, chances are there is a logical fallacy in it. Meaning, no matter how clever it sounds, it has a flaw in the logic that potentially makes what the person is saying, as the Ancient Greeks, Indians and Chinese who pioneered logic would have it, a Crock of Shite. Now, Wikipedia, the last time I checked, listed 114 logical fallacies. They're not all here. If I started to list them all it could become a slippery slope, the floodgates could open and, before you know it, we'd all end up paying more carbon tax (*slippery slope fallacy*).

Knowing these fallacies exist probably won't win you an argument online because people rarely concede victory to those they haven't met. They just go into BLOCK CAPITALS. But it can help you realize you're not going mad and that what they're saying doesn't make full sense – and if they're always at it, then this person is just wasting your time.

Correlation is not causation: just because things happened at the same time doesn't mean one caused the other. For example, Ireland's Eurovision golden era in the early to mid-nineties was also the only time there were four consecutive Ulster winners of the Gaelic football All-Ireland. But there is no evidence that Ulster football is linked to Eurovision success.

Genetic fallacy: ascribing flaws to a person based on their origin. 'Ah, the father was the same.' It's frequently used against TDs, and also against you based on anywhere, really – your parish, your county. Useful for shouting at people from Cork.

Straw man fallacy: where someone deliberately misinterprets something you say to discredit your opinion. Let's say you write, 'I think we should try to do a bit more to preserve nature in rural Ireland.' The straw man reply is 'WHAT? YOU WANT TO PUT FAMILY FARMS OUT OF BUSINESS? CLASSIC GREEN NAZIS.'

If someone avoids your argument by criticizing you, just lash them with Latin. This is an *ad hominem*, or 'against the person', fallacy. 'I DON'T SEE YOU HELPING THE HOMELESS' is shouted at anyone who wants to raise legitimate questions about whether there are right and wrong ways to help homeless people. It's also found in sentences that begin with 'It's all very well for you to talk' and 'Easy for you to say'. 'Easy for you to say' is very easy for you to say, actually. You just find out something about someone then put it at the end of a sentence.

Easy for you to say and you . . .

- living in the city with the public transport

- living in the country with the room to put in a heat pump

- living in a big house

- living in a small house with the small heating bills

- retired

- with your life ahead of you

- with your big car able to carry all that stuff

- with your small car using less fuel

- with your children

- with no children

Whataboutery is a great one. Its official title is the *tu quoque fallacy*. *Tu quoque* is swank for you too. So no matter what you say about what we should do in Ireland, you are wrong because I DON'T SEE YOU TALKING ABOUT CHINA. This should be countered by the Irish Mammy defence, which can cut through any fallacy. This is 'If China jumped off a cliff, would you follow them too?'

A lot of these fallacies appear on social media, the influence of which requires a PhD to deal with. But here's my home-spun philosophy that has made me a lot less angry.

Hey, why not use social media to connect? But also get the fuck off social media

Occasionally I'll trawl through earlier versions of me on social media. I'm surprised at how annoying I was. I was more aggressive. I did more 'calling out' of people. Writing things for popularity and contributing nothing, all in pursuit of this endless goal of Raising Awareness. In the absence of a diary, old social media posts are a great way to, in the words of Rabbie Burns, 'see oursels as ithers see us!' I read and cringe at how I'm appointing myself spokesperson for other people to take a bin company to task for raising their standing charge. It's not the importance of the issue that's the problem: it's the self-importance. The placing myself at the centre of it. At one stage I even tried to instigate a pile-on. Thankfully no one listened because I massively overestimated my importance. I am not qualified enough to change anyone's mind on social media. I do not have any true facts and expertise to bring to the table. But I'm fair to middling at asking questions in, hopefully, mostly a non-knobby way.

So here's what I do now as much as possible.

Just find out

Last spring, after a good bit of driving around the country, I noticed the hedges were more cut than I'd ever seen them. I remember when the roadside ditches around Dripsey were tended by one man with a scythe and a dog. He cleared drains with a shovel. He was constant, unwavering. There wasn't a machine or fourteen lads standing around looking at him. There's still a tasty man with a machine operating in Dripsey but in many places hedges seem to be cut by Optimus Prime. The top of the hedge looks like the cross-section of a Lion Bar – just lots of sawed whitethorns that didn't seem to be doing any harm to anyone.

Or if they do the side, the hedge looks punished. Gashed branches and stalks make it look less like hedge management and more like the hedge is being taught a lesson and made an example of, lest nature get any more bright ideas.

It was depressing. I was annoyed. It looked awful. I asked Twitter why it seemed worse. Lots of people said the same thing. *It's bad. People are bad. They don't give a shite. There is a vendetta against nature.* But there were two other important types of reply: *This is how you manage a hedge – if you let it grow too high it gets leggy, and animals can knock it down.*

Also it's for laying broadband cable.

Now those two replies don't cheer me up because they are just suggestions. But at least a bit of me doesn't feel like Everything Is Shit. There is a reason. And where there are reasons, they can be looked at in isolation without feeling that Humans Are Bad. And where that is a possibility, then I don't feel despair. And the main goal is to keep going and not despair. I don't have the mental energy to take on anyone else's rage, so I thanked people for the responses and my next tweet was something happier. Someone had planted a load of trees. I wanted to tell other people about it.

Spread good news

I've started doing this a bit more. Where people are doing good things – planting trees, making ponds, a new cycle lane – I just try to let others know. Everyone needs a lift.

People need encouragement, and they may be trying to start something within a large organization, to gradually move people along. And if they get praise it'll make their jobs easier. But if they get slated, their sceptical colleagues could point and say, 'I don't know why you bother. Some people are never happy.'

A new parking-protected cycle lane was put in near the Phoenix Park during Covid. It was part of a general installation of cycle lanes that made it feel like they were in a rush to get stuff done before some bollox came back into the office and noticed. Parking-protected cycle lanes in Ireland – though normal in many countries – seem almost revolutionary. We had no concept of not cycling pinned between a bus and someone's wing-mirror. So when these came in I nearly started talking in Danish while passing through them. I posted a photo on social media in joy and the majority of the replies were sniping that the surface was rough and it wasn't wide enough.

And I'm thinking, *I KNOW, but can we at least try to acknowledge a first step?*

There are farmers growing nettles for corncrakes and plots for skylarks. There are people with tiny backyards seeing a bird. There is joy there. Someone else can share the bad news for a while.

Assume non-asshole until further proof

Sometimes I get abuse. That's easy. *Bye*. I looked it up in the terms and conditions and it turns out I'm not employed by The World to reply. Sometimes they seem cranky but not immediately abusive, so I look at how they're replying to other things to see whether they're a knob or that's just Their Way. I reply politely, and if the next one is dickish, I just leave them be. I mute and never see them again and it's amazing. My brain forgets them and the world has not ground to a halt because this conversation has stopped.

Others are watching

I don't mean that in a creepy way. Although there are a few of those too. But interacting on social media about th'environment and climate change and whatnot is not just about you. It's not just about whoever you're replying to, hopefully having an amazing meeting of minds and not calling each other pricks. It's about the people watching. If your argument is sound but you're being a bit of a dick, people watching might not buy your argument. I'm not saying you shouldn't get angry like Jennifer Lawrence in *Don't Look Up*. Do. Go for it. But if you were also hoping to drag a few others along with you, maybe see if what you're about to write will have them flocking to your side or will they just look away and think, *Do I really want the hassle?*

Grow up a small bit

It is both astonishing to see how childish people are on social media and also not even a little surprising because it's so easy.

I'm not expecting plaudits, but you wouldn't believe the shite I've stopped myself writing. Just pure petulance. Bernard Metzler, an American radio personality, said, 'Before you speak ask yourself if what you are going to say is true, is kind, is necessary, is helpful. If the answer is no, maybe what you are about to say should be left unsaid.' Now, obviously the most important thing for me is *Is it funny?* But I've discarded a rake of things because they weren't funny enough to justify breaking a few of those rules. It's not being holier than thou. It's being selfish. When I tweeted when annoyed, I'd spend ages replying and worrying. Now I don't give my unsaid words a moment's thought.

Occasionally, I relapse and just put the boot in along with everyone else or snap back at someone, adding fuel to a fire. But mainly I save it in the drafts. You're not being paid for this. No one cares. Some people have nothing else to do except wait for things to reply to. Lots of people don't live their lives on social media and seem the better for it. Grow up.

That's my instruction to myself. I had written something a lot worse, but I left it in the drafts.

It's fascinating

I learn so much from social media. I have stopped just feeling depressed about all the bad news. Either I'm immune, fatalistic, hopeful that some things can be done or getting less angry so it takes less out of me, but on any given day I'll know a bit more about whether it's worth my while getting a heat pump or solar panels or how do you make a pond or why you need to cut rushes to help hen harriers or how to turn off an electric fence with your phone, what the Younger Dryas was and why that's not relevant to climate change, no matter what your friend on Facebook says, or how to build a berm to help flood a bog or how to feel about buddleia.

I don't have to have the last word

And finally, the last word. One of the benefits of the passage of time is realizing I know nothing. It has been tremendously liberating to say, 'Okay, I didn't know that. Thanks.' And then ... here's the magic bit ... Move on. Can you believe that?

Of course, that's all very well for me to say because ...

9.

Where do they
get their energy?

'Get out the chequebook there,
Mama, the oil man is here'

– Dada, when the oil man was there

The oil man. Summoned after the dip-stick showed there were only a few inches left. The Campus oil man gave the amount. Mama did a quick sum to work out the price per litre. They'd check the diary to see what was paid the last time and how long ago. Hmmm. A judgement was made. *That's not too bad.* Or *That's gone up.* Dada might mention Iran or Saddam Hussein. Life would go on.

Either way, it wasn't going to be drill, baby, drill. The oil fed the Wellstood, an at-least-sixty-year-old range that has been ever present in the kitchen – so ubiquitous that when I came home from school one day and Cooker Man (a man from Clonakilty who was reputed to be the only man who still fixed them) had the Wellstood pulled out from the wall, it affected me so much I think it'll come up in therapy. It wasn't just the motor fuel my parents watched like a hawk. My father and mother were rigid with the home heating oil for the range. Forget your fancy heat pumps. Just light a cast-iron range early in the morning, turn it off mid-morning when the hot water cylinder was full and let the heat from the range ebb into the room. There was no shower and no immersion. The cylinder was the day's hot water so don't even *think* of taking one of those baths that come up around your shoulders. You're not Pam Ewing.

The other room was heated by an open fire with timber from the farm. The upstairs was heated by hot-water bottles and 120-watt heaters called the Human Body. I wouldn't call it fuel poverty. It was more 'character building'. The fuel was out in the tank if it was really needed – say, if we had visitors. Although, famously, one visitor misunderstood the terms of reference for the bath and had a full one and took all the hot water. There was a shadow over the rest of their visit.

I moved to Dublin where there was central heating. I would press a switch and it would come on and the house was warm. And I forgot just how much of a big deal that was. It's easy to forget where you get your energy.

The Joule of Denial

I don't want to get all woo-woo, *wellness is about positive attitude, you can buy these crystals from my Instagram page,* but energy is everything and everything is energy. Even the renewable energy that your electricity provider said was green, with pictures of windmills in the ads and people with good teeth smiling as they boiled the kettle and a flaxen-haired child running up to them to show them a drawing and it was gorgeous – even that electricity is mixed with all the dirty stuff so that sometimes you're not actually using green electricity. You're using methaney stuff. Sorry. They lied. Well, they didn't lie. They just didn't tell you that the electricity they generate is renewable, but that's not always the electricity they send to you. Basically, that's not a bunch of organic carrots. It's a bunch of carrots that are sometimes organic.

Everything you do is a choice to use energy, to turn something that was just sitting there into a thing or a piece of light, heat, entertainment or transport, and that will put CO_2 into the atmosphere. Because all the renewable things we can do with the nice technology will need fossil fuels to be burned to get us to that stage.

I'm not saying this to make you feel bad. We're all doing it just by sitting here with this book or audiobook. A decision made by me based on a combination of good intentions, ego and feeling like I've done something.

But if we *really* want to change things we have to a) change most systems and b) be LESS: do less, make less, consume less, waste less, go less, have less nice. But not less books. That's a red line. But the main red line is that people who have less should pay less.

Those who can, should

The richer you are, the bigger your carbon footprint has been. Sorry, I don't make the rules. Not you, I know *you've* a passive house, but it's the other fella on the other side of the mews. The one who hasn't switched over to the electric Range Rover yet, like you have. But even if the poorer family is still burning kerosene in the Paraglo, basically inhaling most of the CO_2 themselves, and not using the heat pump like you are, statistically, they are just living a lower-carbon existence. Richer people fly more and further, ski more, have more cars per person, own more appliances, go on more stags to Tallinn, stay in more hotels, have bigger houses to heat and bigger immaculate lawns, more clothes, jewellery and those weird aluminium-looking bottles, are more likely to work in jobs that contribute no good to the world whatsoever but involve trading imaginary units of wealth around the place and incentivizing shareholder value and meeting KPIs in the Customer Joy Vertical.

So those here who don't have much should pay less to fix it. They should still pay more than the average person in Suriname. But definitely less than those with money here. So we need what's called a Just Transition. The idea is that in order to change an entire economy away from fossil fuels towards one that's less dig-it-up-and-burn-it you have to do a few things right.

- Transitioning doesn't mean a few already-rich people hoover up all the benefits.

- People who had jobs that are now suddenly not-cool need to be re-skilled and they need help finding jobs and they need money while all of this is happening.

- People who are marginalised because of money have to be represented and included when it comes to deciding how to change Everything about an economy.

Even as I type Just Transition I feel that its time as a phrase may not be long. We have a habit of associating a phrase with some other rage we're feeling and before long the phrase has to be quietly left out. So just so you know, Just Transition did mean something.

Words speak louder than actions

Certain words and phrases have been chewed up and misused so much that their original meaning has been forgotten. They've become so charged that to use them now means people on either side will stop listening. They might be triggered. (Apologies for those triggered by the use of the word *triggered*. I know it can be a triggering word for those who think we're gone too soft on words. I should have really issued a *trigger* trigger warning.)

Political correctness might be the grandparent of them all. Variously it has been used to describe policies by Nazis, then communists, then the right thing to do politically, then as an in-joke among different communists, then anything the Left does, and it continued to evolve so that now being anti-PC means anything from *I'm not a racist but . . .* to not eating leafy vegetables.

Woke started as an African-American term about being politically aware nearly a hundred years ago but now is used as a criticism of . . . nearly everything. Seriously, if you google *woke* and almost any noun you'll find a news story where one side is accused of being woke. I tried it with things that were next to me on the desk: tea-bags, bread, a mug. Each one popped up a story.

Well, into this mess I'd like to bring back *check your privilege*. This is relatively new and meant 'before you open your big mouth, take a few minutes to see whether your opinion is influenced by the fact that, relatively speaking, Things Are Fine for You'. But then it became a slogan, and people got angry because they felt they were being asked to acknowledge something they were sure they didn't have.

But still it's handy. I need to check my privilege, and if you don't like it, look away for a bit.

I'm doing it because it's incredibly annoying when someone is harping on about what needs to change and it turns out they won't have to make too many sacrifices. So I'm being upfront about it now. Or at least before the end of the book. Just so you know I'm aware. For all the good that'll do.

First up, when it comes to privilege, the entire premise of this book is covered in the stuff. I am worried about climate change and the death of so much of the natural world. I would like to do something but am bewildered about how to do the right thing personally and how to help bring about systematic change. As well as still being unwilling to make huge changes.

Well, diddums, it's a privilege to be able to fret in a vague way about what I might do. There are hundreds of millions of people for whom this stuff is already happening. They are dying in 50-degree heatwaves, their farms are dust, militia are killing them for water, they need to leave to save their lives, some countries might disappear under the sea, one might lose access to its sea because of weapons paid for by fossil fuels sold to cuddly friendly European countries.

In my lifetime, this country might become a bit drier at times, with heavier rain, stronger winds, more spring forest and gorse fires, but roughly it'll still be liveable. In the global scheme of things, we'll probably be grand and, who knows, maybe we'll grow rich in an unscrupulous future selling wave energy and harvested rain to the highest bidder. Although that might get us invaded/liberated.

I am not immediately worried about my livelihood. I think I'll be able to get by in most versions of the future. I have no job, just a series of gigs based on relationships. I have no premises, large equipment that I've borrowed for this job. No one is asking me to make revolutionary changes to how I make money. Yet.

I have a family who I care about and who care about me and a community who thus far haven't made any formal complaints to the police. I feel included and represented. Again, this is something I take for granted. Not everyone feels included. When you're excluded, everything is more work.

As a man, there is some shit I don't have to deal with. I get less abuse online than women who are comedians or writers or who write about the environment. I get abuse but typically it's people who think I'm wrong, a gobshite, but none that threaten harm or insult the entire basis of my being. If I'm getting cross with a van driver, it's as a man. I could still get a slap but it's a different fear.

When I blithely suggest more cycling, I do so as a man. I have been assaulted on a bicycle a few times. Once by young lads throwing things and the other time by a fella off his head on something. Or just dead inside. It was hard to tell from his eyes as he hit me while opening a rear taxi door and then accused me of not paying tax. That stopped me in my tracks. I was all set to ask which tax period he was referring to specifically and if we could make an amended return when he pulled me off the bike.

But it's not the constant dread that women and girls experience from motorists and others because of who they intrinsically are, not because they encountered an asshole.

I am white in a country that is overwhelmingly white. I spend approximately zero minutes wondering if the person approaching me on the street is going to reference my skin colour. It's one less thing I have to do. Someone might disparagingly say 'Meh, cis-white-male-typical-pffft' but it doesn't really affect me. My demographic has a long tradition of Things Being Fine to fall back on.

I am healthy. Maintaining my health is cheap at the moment. I am not dependent on a hospital waiting list.

I currently have no additional mobility needs, so when I advocate for space for more people-friendly cities, I am automatically thinking about me, walking and cycling, as opposed to someone who is blind or uses a wheelchair or a walker. I briefly experienced it with a child buggy, but unless there are any other issues, we grew out of that.

I don't suffer fuel or food poverty. I don't dislike my job most of the time, and I am not trapped in it.

I have no mental health issues, apart from crippling self-doubt, inability to focus and spending too much time doom-scrolling. But other than that, I get by. I am not grieving the recent loss of a loved one.

The point of this is not breast-beating or cloak-rending or I'm-sorry-for-being-so-lucky. It's just to say I have the capacity to say something stupid about What Needs To Be Done without realizing how it affects others, but also the capacity to spend time learning a bit and hopefully helping a bit.

Not everyone does. That's why if you have a bit of spare capacity or time, ask yourself if there's anything you can do. It doesn't mean that if you are stretched by any challenges that you have to opt out. More so that others should have your back, and you're welcome if you can make it, the meeting's at eight, but we'll send around notes after if you can't get there. So that's why I check my privilege. That wasn't so hard, was it?

So every word out of anyone's mouth about what we need to do to protect the environment needs to be accompanied by the same amount of words about how we protect anyone whose income, access, housing or opportunities are less than the average. Otherwise we're not going to get the unity we need to work together.

Covid proved what we can achieve when we work together, but also how we're not in it together. Covid was the *Room Raiders* blacklight for Ireland. You got to see all the stains of how our economy works. We just about hung together for that because we figured it wouldn't go on forever and there were signs we were headed in the right direction. Numbers that showed there were results.

If we don't make our decarbonization or rebuilding of nature fair for people it won't get support and then people will think the 'Green Agenda' is just a 'load of bollox' and set fire to the mountains whether they need to or not. I can foresee a situation where cutting down a tree (for the hell of it and not for necessity) will be an act of rebellion. An act of rebellion by a gobshite, to be sure, but still a rebel in some people's eyes.

We need to listen to what people on low incomes care about. What are the catch-22s and binds of poverty that simply do not affect someone with enough money? That'll tell you where the systematic issues are much faster than your struggle to find spelt. Where can they get fruit and veg – do they have a butcher nearby? What are the brands they have to buy and why? How much do they spend on the basics? Who built the houses they live in? How much heat is leaking out through the window-frames? Is there a bus? How far is it to cycle? How does it feel to be 'nudged' towards a different mode of transport if the mode isn't there and you're poor? Does it feel like a sharp nudge in the teeth? Taking out the carbon while taking the piss is not sustainable. Every single thing is energy. And the less money you have, the more you are aware of that. When you travel, heat your house, worry about whether your job is still part of the plan.

So if you have any, check your privilege. But we don't have much time so don't spend all day at it. It's not next to your navel.

10.

TBH, I'm not able after all of that

Turn on the news there.
Even if we know it's all bad news.

– Dada asking for the news to be turned on

There's a lot to think about. Don't forget to give yourself a break.

An Intergovernmental Panel on Climate Change (IPCC) report came out in 2022. I've read the summary and every now and then I dip into the full report. It's longer than the latest Hilary Mantel. That's where we're at now. Comedians reading 3,600-page climate-change reports.

It's huge, not just in pages. My bits of rubbish, bit of cycling, few trees planted – what difference does it make compared to the sheer scale of the problem?

What is the point, like? What is the point in carrying any of this emotional baggage? It's like worrying about the death of the universe. It's going to happen. It mightn't affect me. No one will know if I do anything or not. Just being a normal person and living your life and not trying to 'do your bit' is not in any way wrong. But it's sort of too late. I'm hooked now.

First of all, I just wallow for a bit and then give myself ah-fuckit moments, without guilt. While writing this, there's a rake of other stuff I could be doing instead. But ah-fuckit, I can't do everything. And also some ah-fuckit moments of driving, consumption, getting a thing on Amazon, eating a filthy bit of food that's dripping possible animal misery. I have to say the a-effit-word from time to time.

Ah-fuckit doesn't mean throwing up your hands in despair and throwing your broken fridge into a ditch. That requires planning, help, scouting before eventually ah-fuckiting the Beko into the area of special conservation and finch habitat. Throwing the appliance off the wagon is not falling off the wagon. It's different, it's destructive. Ah-fuckiting is just taking a holiday from the endless thinking. And any guilt.

But then I drag myself back on the horse. Send that email to the billboard company asking if they won't mow the strip of grass they own around it and will leave it for the pollinators, and if they forget, ah-fuckit. It'll grow again. And I'll send another email.

And despair? My little bits and pieces, making a few people laugh around the country, writing, planting, picking, tentatively starting out on something I might do for the rest of my life – it could be wiped out in a second by one oligarch backing his yacht into a better parking spot, one nearer the Spar. One time there was a rare snail in Kildare that delayed a bypass for two years while they figured out how to preserve its habitat. As well as the building-delay costs, no doubt, the cars stuck in bottleneck traffic during those two years travelled at less efficient speeds and burned more carbon (which, in theory, should lead to people making public transport and mixed-mode transport choices but, because it's Ireland, everyone just sat in their cars and fumed because the trains were too packed). For a six-million-euro delay and adjustment they saved the snail, and then the following winter, flooding from heavy rain killed nearly all the snails anyway.

So what was the point? I can't speak for this project, but I *think* the point was that in trying they learned. About snails, bypasses, floods, Kildare, swearing, the skills of others. You show you care. Caring is important. It influences others to care. You hope you'll win this battle, but if not you'll know better for the next one. Isn't life mainly small islands of victory between oceans of annoyance? You're not comparing your situation to an idealized situation, where everything had gone right. You're comparing it to if you had done nothing at all.

You'll hear people talking about global temperature rises and how we've lost the battle to keep the rise at 1.5 degrees and we hope it won't be 2 degrees and maybe it'll get to 1.8 degrees, and it can seem like not a lot of degrees, but we're talking about the entire planet. So there's a lot hidden in the averages: 1.5 is a lot, 0.5 is a lot, 0.3 is a lot. In fact, every point-something is a lot. Even point-zero-something is a hell of a lot of extra heat in the giant skin around this giant ball. They're all worth fighting for. Every point-something the temperature doesn't go beyond 1.5 makes a difference for millions of lives, millions of square kilometres, lots of future. Everything is worth fighting for. So take a break, ah-fuckit for a while and get back at it again. And if at the end of all this, the temperature still goes up and the cities are flooded, the hills are on fire and the dolphins are leaving in their escape pods, then we can say, 'Ah-fuckit. At least we tried.' But how hard am I trying?

Tactivist

I have done a bit of comedy at a few environmentally themed events. People want a bit of a laugh as they grapple with serious things. I guess they ask me because I'm not going to tell them WE'RE ALL GOING TO DIE or YOU'LL TAKE MY TURF OVER MY DEAD BODY. They are daytime, sober events in brightly lit function rooms, or even Zoom calls, so it's always going to be hard to get the crowd going. It's hard to do one-liners and gentle ribbing about how decarbonization requires something so systematic that the 200-year-old version of extractive capitalism will have to be completely rebuilt in three years and your carbon trading ideas are probably bullshit and you can't grow your way out of this one with innovation, techman, you need to rethink everything . . . That's just going to be a bit heavy and indigestible in that atmosphere. Or maybe I haven't written the jokes yet. It's pretty light on solutions, but if I can make people laugh without making the One Vegan Joke or HAHA, WE COULD DO WITH GLOBAL WARMING HERE, HAH, SAYS YOU – OH, STOP THE LIGHTS, I

HAD MY BIG COAT ON THIS MORNING in the general area of sustainability, it's at least a bit of light relief for people grappling with huge problems, and if they have a laugh at the event maybe they'll go and do one more thing. Sometimes when I'm introduced, they describe me as a comedian and an *activist*. I don't think I've done enough to deserve the title 'activist' when you look how active real activists are. I don't feel very active. I haven't done any shouting. I haven't protested, put my body on the line or done any politics. And to tell you the truth, I'm afraid. Afraid people will laugh at me in the wrong way. Afraid of ridicule. (Yes, by the way, lots of comedians are afraid of ridicule. Aside from the fact that it's not pleasant, it's because we're not in control of the laughs. Half of us are only doing comedy as a general reaction to some childhood ridicule anyway.)

I'm not saying I won't be an activist. I'm building up to it. But I just want everyone to get along. I think I'm a *tactivist*. I have a vague notion that if people spend civil time together they might come up with solutions that are imperfect and make neither side happy but are a step along the way. I worry I might be fuck-all use. Or doing more harm than good. Gentle ribbing to make the climate-change meet-up a bit more pleasant won't cut it when what we need is a revolution. A fall of the decadent, decaying Roman-empire-type stuff. We need Mad-Max Goths and Huns ruling the roost. Relocate the cities to mountain retreats. Bring back hand-me-down clothes. No one is entitled to a phone upgrade until the puffin population recovers. More blacksmiths, for some reason. People with clothes made from the bonnets of old SUVs. A strange messianic figure called Doctor Light who leads people in a cult that worships solar panels and broken Nutribullet blades.

But while waiting for the Fall of Civilization there's a good few of us who need to work our way into it. People who are not officially working in the area but want to help. People who like writing well-phrased emails and making spread-sheets of rosters for who'll take an apple tree, people who like to build consensus, who'll gently stand up for someone embroiled in a toxic discussion, someone with a printer, someone with a car. Someone who has learned patience the hard way. Who knows that very few things are pointless.

Pointless has a point too

I'll tell ya one thing about raising or minding children. It's a handy mechanism for stealthily developing what I believe to be an underrated but important skill: the ability to do mindless tasks. Tasks for which you generally get no thanks, and the thanks you might get will be far in the future when you'll have to privately take credit because no one will have remembered your role.

You are standing in the middle of a blazing three-way row between two crying little girls about what the name of the mermicorn in the colouring book should be and which of the girls gets to *be* the mermicorn in an elaborate game involving beads and rice crispies and a set of rules as long as a constitution. And you start shouting and then cajoling and in the end give them Maltesers even though it's not the weekend and they'll be up all evening.

No one is watching – it's pointless. You have to pick all the necklace beads out of the cereal like Cinderella with the lentils. But you do it out of love – love is in there somewhere, as you swear loudly – there is no option not to, and your reward is that at the end of the day no one has choked on beads or slapped their sister over a mermicorn name. And cans.

It's a pointless ongoing task. But like everything we do for our families, young or old, there is a compulsion, a stake in the future, that act of love. Even if the little scuts don't know it. Oh, sure, they'll say something vague on the winner's podium (my children will be on podiums, obviously) about how they couldn't have done it without me and my wife, but they won't mention specifically the time I pulled brioche out of the roof of their mouth where it was stuck.

It's not a perfect match, but it is some preparation for point-lessness. Every email to the council about dumping; every minute spent agonizing over the diplomatic phrasing of a group WhatsApp message; every bit of rubbish picked up or tree planted, some of which won't make it because of vandals. Me and another person in the tree-planting group planted six in one 'frontier zone' – I knew we were leaving the trees at the mercy of young lads with a bit of time on their hands. Maybe it was a bit provocative – and, also, who did I think I was thinking trees were what the area needed after a century of neglect? But you live in hope. There's one of them left now. And I love the stubborn little bollox of a tree. It survived having the top of its trunk snapped off . But it's still there. It made one apple last autumn, hanging there alone like it was in WALL-E's fridge. It's not pretty or pictur-esque. I won't be gutted if something happens. It was an act of optimism. There will be more – like those 250 little whips of trees a gang of us planted in two hours. There'll be attrition but it won't take all of them.

What can you do?

First of all, have a look around. Who are your networks? You probably don't call them networks because you're a normal person and it's just Stuff You Do. So start with your family. Families are weird and it can be hard to talk to them honestly, unless it's at a funeral and you're all hammered, but you never know what might happen if you start a conversation. Getting people to say out loud what they've only said in a Facebook comment at least gets it out into the open. And rather than jumping down anyone's throat, just gently say, 'Oh yeah . . . I read a thing there that says the kettle is the most energy intensive bit of a cup of tea, even more than getting the tea here from India – isn't that a good one?' and then walk away.

Take it handy with them. People – especially family – get very sensitive if they think you're criticizing their way of doing things. But there'll be times when some meme that originated in a Milwaukee far-right gun-lobby group will infiltrate the sanctity of the Family Including Mam WhatsApp group via a cousin via the Priest's Petrol Money Collection Rota Group, and you might be called upon to gently debunk it. 'Actually, yeah, I saw that too but, no, Greta never told the Chinese not to use chopsticks.'

You can learn the joys of reverse image search, where you find something on social media being shared by someone who does a lot of stuff about guardian angels, but when you look it up, you discover the rubbish was not left behind by teenage climate activists but did, in fact, come from the 1994 UEFA Cup Final fan zone.

Is a child in the family big into all of this? You don't have to do anything – just encourage them. Give them a spin somewhere that's important to them in all of this. YES, IN THE CAR IF YOU HAVE TO. We might have to burn a bit of diesel to turn this around.

If the family are just not into it, who's outside? Sports, church, school? Are people leaving the engine running outside of the school? Are the school clamping down on children going to climate strikes? Fuck 'em. Write to them and say COP ON. What difference does missing one double French and accounting after lunch make? I say that now, of course, because MY children are not doing the Leaving Certificate at the moment. We'll see if my tune has changed if I think they're going to miss out on university points. Maybe I'll be marching them *straight back into that school if there's any sign of slippage in the mocks*. But I'd like to think I'll be supportive. And they can always repeat.

Is there a WhatsApp group 'Doing a Bit' in the local area? Is it currently one legend who's overworked and doesn't know what to do next because it's a bit overwhelming? Might you be the second/third/fourth person in high-vis to join? Because in the future there may be a community energy project or community composting, and this is the network that forms the basis of it. Tiny grams of carbon here or there. Your community influences the next one over. They're wondering how ye got the district heating plant for yere zone. (I'm getting carried away now – I don't know how long it'll be before we'll have a massive heat pump on a street-corner site that pumps heat to five small houses, but you never know.) But community composting is already happening. Might you start it in your area?

When there's an election, candidates will know – this area is Never Not At It. This area gives a shit. We'd better have some policies. We'd better not be sending in any gobshite who can't tell the difference between weather and climate to be the candidate. And, no, I'm not telling you who to vote for. I'm saying that by demanding more from the candidates you *might* get better candidates. No guarantee. But you'll get shag-all if you don't ask.

Are you a farmer or in another industry that's feeling a bit beaten up by the conversation? Feeling accused? I know I said before we don't time for your feelings but we have a little bit of time. I understand you. There have been times when comedians have been lambasted and same-brush-tarred. But you, the people with land, machinery, hitches on your vehicles. YOU HAVE TRACTORS. You're the people who help out during floods with transport and septic-tank cleaners and St Patrick's Day parades and bring Christmas trees to the crossroads and teleporters for the Christmas lights and a load of earth for the new wildflower bank. You use literal horsepower to make changes on your land. Of course, you won't get the thanks for it. No one might see the pond you dig or the hedges you plant now, but one day someone will. The lovely grove of mixed native trees will peep over a shed. They'll see a hen harrier tear out of it after a rat. There might be grants or there might not. But you could be the link in a bit of habitat that connects one patch of ground to a ring fort. One day someone will remember that and say your name and say, 'I think it was them who planted that – fair fucks.' That's all we want – to feel that one day someone will say 'fair fucks'.

A few years after he died, people still liked my father because of bits and bobs he did around the place. They PUT UP A SEAT TO HIM in Dripsey near one of his fields. Can you believe how chuffed he'd be that people put up a lovely seat to him? He wasn't a hero. He was just a nice man who tipped away, planting trees for people.

I don't know what kind of WhatsApper he'd have been. Pure nosy, I hope. If you do find yourself in a local WhatsApp group, just be careful. We are not built for the stress of weaponized text. Try to only bring actions and good news to the group.

These all sound like individual actions and, of course, it's still a hundred companies doing 70 per cent of the bad stuff and YEAH, CHINA but whoever we are, we will have to cut back on our fossil fuels and our clothes and our gadgets and our travelling and our most energy-intensive food.

Of course, this all sounds like the personal-responsibility thing, a clever trick the fossil-fuel industry paid PR companies to push so we'd feel guilty and not demand big change. It isn't. My point is that when you are half-arsed like me, not naturally campaigny, the changes you make yourself or the small bits of volunteering you do act as a training ground. You meet people. They tell you things. You get depressed because you're getting nowhere, but all you have to do is

Not. Fuck. Off. Just hang in there until a job or task or bit of a change comes up that's more your thing. And while you're hanging in there, keep an eye on . . .

The media

Yes, the media. What are you doing? You – unspecified media person with a bit of a following and influence. Are you doing a bit? You have 100,000 listeners on local radio or 200,000 on national radio. Are you helping? Is your mid-morning matters show sponsored to the hilt by someone who fears change because it affects their bottom line? Are you okay with that? Are you facilitating, in the interests of 'balance', someone who is not an expert and is just on the air TO WASTE FUCKING TIME WE DON'T HAVE? To say, 'That's all very well, but the Dublin media don't know what's going on down the country,' yet they don't bring a solution? Are your guests the same people as you, all trained by the same PR company, for whom politics and policy are a game, just an extension of university debating? Or are you bringing in new experts, new voices, people who know about farming and wildlife, van driving and carbon reduction? Are you having debates that end up with people shouting over each other or actually productive conversations where acknowledging new information is not a sign of having been OWNED in the debate? We. Don't. Have. Time. For. This. Shit. Are you replacing fact with opinion?

Big media people with your money made already – why not think about your legacy now? You won't have time to spend your money, so now is your chance to do something. We need the rich to do more than everyone else because they have the money to make the time. Especially those with charisma, communications skills – c'mon! Ask someone – an expert, not me – how you can help.

Magazine – is your psychology slot about how to help people to get through despair and apathy about this? Are you 'generating heat' just for clicks? Interviewing someone thoughtful and balanced and then picking an inflammatory headline out of context just to get hackles raised, so no one on the fence will approach the thing with an open mind but you'll get clicks for the luxury-SUV company sponsoring the ad next to the piece? Or on the radio, *again, for balance*, reading out texts from members of the public who are not random but are mobilized to scotch the argument with COMPLETE BULLSHIT as somehow representative of the person on the street? WE DON'T HAVE TIME FOR THIS SHIT. Stop it! If it were a war would you be Tucker Carlsoning? Or would you post numbers where people can find shelters and donate blankets?

This is a battle to save the planet. Your thirty-year-old way of making media isn't good enough. No matter who is sponsoring the programme. Speaking of which . . .

Companies

I know many of you have sustainability programmes and a beehive and keep-cups and a drinking fountain. But you know your whole point of existence is to burn vast amounts of fossil fuels to make shit we don't really need, right? You know that, don't you? Like, you can carbon trade all you want out of that. You can say you've bought a forest in Bolivia and, to the best of your knowledge, no one's logging it, even though it might actually be better for Bolivians to get the money and manage the forest themselves for food and forestry, but, okay, you have your credits and your corporate social-responsibility day where you came out and picked up rubbish with us – and don't get me wrong, we were delighted to see you, but we're already wrestling with the futility of rubbish picking. Is there any way you could just say, 'Actually, look, here's the thing. We're not really doing anything and we're afraid of going out of business. What else could we do with all this kit and these clever people? We're open to suggestions, and we can probably do a bit of changing – not too much in year one because the share price will tank, but keep nagging us.' It would save you a rake of money in PR. What we need now is a reduction in cynicism. And, look – I've taken the money too from time to time. I needed it. I'll still present your CSR award, but maybe we could just be honest with each other.

Within large companies are lots of people who are trying to green them and believe changes can be made. I heard one activist describe what happened following a sit-in at a climate-change-laggard insurance company (insurance companies are VITAL in climate change because they insure fossil-fuel sites – if an oil well can't get insurance it won't drill). After the sit-in, employees contacted the activists saying, 'Thank you. It's easier to raise this stuff now after you put the pressure on.' In transport departments and foresters and seed companies and metalworking firms, just get rid of the word sustainability and say, 'Look – we burn shit to make shit. Here are some good things. The rest, we don't know how to change. Yet.'

And let's start from there.

I wouldn't open with it

In comedy, the saying 'I wouldn't open with it' refers to a joke that either isn't funny enough or is difficult to get across. And I really believe that, when it comes to engaging as many people as possible, first impressions last.

Remember, changing an entire planet's atmospheric make-up and stopping extinction means trying to change *everything*. But you don't have to *start* with everything.

You might be the first person to have this type of conversation with someone. So I would suggest you don't start by telling them their daffodils are actually no use to bees. Say, 'Aren't them daffodils lovely?' And then mention the other wildflowers that might work *too*. Don't be digging up their first efforts.

A volunteer came with us on a clean-up for the first time. She was asking about planting bulbs and we were tentatively thinking about doing a bit, but no one had time and the turnouts weren't great and we needed a few more people. She said, 'What about there?' pointing to a place. And a person from the group she'd never spoken to before – gone now (left, I haven't had them disappeared or anything; we're not a militant group . . . yet) – just snapped back that there was no point. Foxes would dig them out straight away. The woman's face fell, her suggestion battered into the ground like a well-trodden Prazsky can. And I never saw her at another clean-up again.

Please, please, please, when someone comes in with suggestions and all enthusiastic – unless they're suggesting tar sands – just let them have their say. Accept the bid. I couldn't give a fuck if the fox digs up the bulbs or not. He can dig them up and shout NERDS at us. I don't care. Thank you for your suggestion, nice woman, and maybe we'll plant the bulbs, and if the fox digs them up that's just bad karma for the fox. Maybe a swan will break his arm.

Now, I can't say for definite that a person would leave just because of that. Maybe they had a flight to Bulbville booked anyway. But whoever you are, wherever you are, come back. We'll plant whatever you want.

Similarly if you're trying to persuade a council or a company or a government or a family member or a neighbour to let nature take its course, in the words of an old saying I just made up: don't necessarily start with ragwort. We had complaints about an area we wanted left wild. They complained about ragwort. Ragwort triggers some sort of memory in everyone of poison and neglect. And it's illegal, sort of. We haven't had time to get the image-makers in to help, so for now, cinnabar moths, I'm sorry. We'll delay but eventually pull the ragwort. This year. Maybe next year there'll be a heartwarming video on *Ellen* about ragwort and 'Why People Now Love Ragwort' articles everywhere, but for now, we're not opening with it.

Don't have the hard battle first.

Aren't they all green politicians now?

Anyone who is a green politician has put in far more hard hours than I have. They are most likely qualified in this area and, if not, the sheer amount of abuse they have taken far outweighs what others get, perhaps because the entire raison d'être of their career is to actually change things. Regardless of the compromises along the way, at some point there was an actual ideology.

And they get into government, which means they will undoubtedly disappoint. From larger parties, people expect competence but no real change. They don't expect an ideology apart from more of the same plus a few tweaks.

So when the green politician disappoints no more than the average politiciany disappointment, the fall is hard. It's emotional. There is betrayal.

I don't particularly feel betrayed. I think you try some shit. It works. You swallow some terrible compromises. You get some stuff through. I'm not happy, but I'm not betrayed. And I definitely don't think they are that detached from rural Ireland. Ireland is 300 miles wide. How detached could you be? It's not America. It's not the difference between the DC beltway and a corrugated iron shack in the badlands of the Dakotas, three time zones away.

Maybe a green politician will become moot anyway. With the seas boiling, it won't matter who is who – we'll just be in survival mode.

But for the time we have left to change direction, or at least stop things getting worse – three years, according to the

IPCC – can I just ask one thing of green politicians? And it goes for anyone making statements.

It is clear that how the message is delivered is as important as the message now. Can you just get someone to read it first who is not part of your network – someone miles away? Why not pay someone who is actually struggling financially, give them cold hard cash, to look over a statement? To think about unintended consequences?

No throwaway remarks. Don't go on social media to rant to make yourself feel better. Leave it in the drafts.

We have so little time left to change habits, systems, we need as many people on board as possible. Everyone. Not just the converted. We need the suspicious, the disgruntled, annoyed, pissed off, out of pocket, status threatened, the people for whom the changes being suggested are life changing, to still say, 'It sticks in my craw but I know it has to be done. I don't like them but I understood what they were saying, and I suppose we'd better crack on with it.'

What is a tragedy is if we waste time arguing politics. Green politicians may deserve your impatience and disappointment – vote them to hell the next time if you want – but the message will still be the same. Most of the time all they're telling us is just physics. Might as well hear it from them as anyone else.

And the rest of the politicians – if the greens are not doing their job, you need to do their job. Not a different job. There is only one job. Grow up and do it. Be a leader. Be greener than the green politician. They'd be delighted if you were. If you play politics with this, future generations will remember you like Billy Zane in *Titanic*. A useless snide bollox. Why not go down fighting like Jack, freezing and clinging to a door, a nudey painting and a romp in an old car planted in your mind?

Not finished

Sometimes great environmental campaigning is done by proper experts who have undergone complete transformation in their lives. They have a before and an after. A busy city life that was, on the face of it, fulfilling. *But something was missing.* So they sat down one day with spouse and children, Skip and Little Mo, as well as Flumper the dog. And they decided something had to change. Their lives were consumptive, extractive, the pace was too fast. They are driven, single-minded, principled. They learn all sorts of country skills. They have taken a leap and the results are there for all to see. They are neutral. They are sequestering. They are a rapidly growing whirlpool into which carbon is being sucked.

That is not me. Clearly, this has not been one of these books. This is a book for the wishy-washy but, in the words of Sun Tzu, even wishy-washy has a bit of solids in it. I ain't transformed nothin'. I've just started. I'll be doing it for the rest of my life, hopefully. I don't know if I'll ever see any results. I'm even looking forward to finishing this fecking book so I can do more of the stuff I keep talking about doing. Because we don't know how much time we have left to do something.

What Dada did next

Dada went sudden in the end. For the last while, he'd gone into himself a small bit. Just tired. Men who labour for seventy years just get worn out. The lungs might have had a bit wrong with them, the kind of disease people who work without masks in dusty outhouses or building sites or factories get. You could tell from the funeral people just liked him. He wasn't a drinker so no one was reminiscing about hoolies or capers or heavy nights below in the pub. Even the age – 84, a good age, a pleasing age. Still, relatively speaking, a tank of a man. A gentleman and a gentle man. He once stopped a fella who was walking the road outside the farm one night and bade him look at the sunset. Just for the look of it. The farm is still there, though the yard is overgrown. In some ways, the farm as it stands now is the perfect representation of Dada's twin aspirations – tasty farming and nature. Our neighbours have it rented. One strong farmer uses the long field for grazing. Nothing has changed there in a while. Glossy cows with plenty of dung. Rich grass. Another outfit from across the valley have the other two main fields. They are a professional operation with machinery Dada would have gazed in admiration at. If the three tractors we owned – the grey Ferguson from 1965, the red Massey, even the Ford 4000 – were next to them, they'd look like those sheepdog-sized *Eohippus* next to Clydesdales. A huge operation. Efficient, big machinery. Years ago Dada worked with their father as a contractor, around the same time as his washing-soda-selling days. (I would have *loved* to know what kind of salesman he was. I would have bought anything. I'd say he was an amazing market researcher, if the data was all about who was building the house over the road.)

The big field is ploughed deep and each year the field does its job. I don't know about soil health or worms or dung beetles, but each year tons of grain and bales come out of it. But the edges. I love to wander off the professional field into the mess at the edges. I don't want to get too grandiose, but there is something quite moving about watching nature reclaim a bit of land. It's moving in every way. There's a part of the hillside where me and Dada and my brothers planted spuds one year by hand because it was too steep for a tractor. A troublesome hill and a hoor to water. In a strange hundred-year circle, the bits that have been rewilded are the bits that were always hard to farm, just like in Gougane Barra, where a state forest covers what used to be farmland. But it's also humming with wildlife. I mean, you have to look a bit for it. You're not going to see a lynx stalk an antelope or a bear body-slam a passing moose. This is small wildlife. A few cinnabar moths hugging a bit of ragwort. Gall mites in the oak trees that presumably get eaten by something up the food chain. Pandas one day, maybe.

A man has horses in the Inch for some of the year. Old grass, dung, dragonflies, damsons, apparently an otter once and the burbling of the river. Some lovely ditch-ash had to be cut because of dieback, but other than that little has changed. It's another haven. I saw buzzards there last summer for the first time in my life. They were probably there before but Mr Naturalist-All-of-a-Sudden wasn't really looking properly. The girls saw them too. I acted all nonchalant when listening to a pair of birds of prey mew (the actual term for a buzzard's cry – I'm getting carried away now). But against a blue sky, to see them gliding looking for prey on the ground (they probably also saw me checking my phone for the correct term for a buzzard's cry) makes me shiver involuntarily. I am in my own little documentary.

A beech fell into the field from the riverbank and was left alone. It stayed alive and now rests on the ground, all its previously lateral southern branches growing upwards like new trunks, as if promoted and delighted with the extra responsibility. It has the effect of making the tree look like it's reclining with its arms in the air ordering more grapes. And beyond is Mary's Bog. We haven't explored it yet with the girls. I hope they too will get their feet stuck in a boghole and call me a bastard. Except we'll get it TikToked, go viral and then face a backlash. The circle of life.

We don't get any money for the scrubby untidy bits. We haven't applied. I'm sure we'd take it if we got it. I'm certainly happy with their general wildness for their own sake. Makes me feel a little less guilty about some other sin I'm committing elsewhere. But what I like most about it is that no one is getting kicked off any land. Food is grown on one bit. Nature grows on the other bit. It has value and no one's arguing. I feel it would offend Dada and the farmers who farm it after to rewild all the land after all the work he put into it.

I might plant a bit of hedge but only with consultation and expertise. There are more trees within the boundaries now than there ever were.

The haggard is quiet. The sheds creak away with age. Butterflies throng the long grass between them. Pigeons and swallows compete to see who can shite more on the old seed drill and broken trailer and pile of timber. The place is saturated with memories and my own two children move among those memories as if Grandad Patsy, who they never met, is still there. There are fifty-year-old bits of work that they ask about. Did Grandad Patsy build that? The span from his past to their future seems like millenia. But what a story that century could span. The breaking and mending of a planet.

At the end of the day – or the End of Days – what else would you be doing?

And ultimately . . . this is the greatest story ever told. How potentially society, for no other reason than it was the right thing to do, slowly, painfully, sometimes quickly and very painfully, turned an enormous tanker around to remake itself as a safer, fairer, less damaging, less awful to nature place to be. How it repaired AN ENTIRE FUCKING ATMOSPHERE. An entire ecosystem. How we brought thirty bird and ninety bee species back from the dead. How we brought the wolf – Okay, we won't start with wolves. How barren mountains that just had sheep are now covered with ribbons of gorgeous furze and willow and oak *and also sheep*, whose wool – currently almost worthless on the market – is used as mulch to help some planted trees grow. How communities have networks for reuse, composting, energy, lobbying local government and companies. And you were a part of that. And then one year you had to take a step back because you were tired of getting nowhere, but you came back and you did this, even though you didn't have to because you'd be dead before the methane bombs were scheduled to hit (the methane burp, a massive release of poisonous methane from ocean sediment sparked by 6-degree climate change, has been debunked, but it got our attention a few years ago, so just checking you're awake). You were doing it entirely for your grandchildren, for other people's grandchildren, for the grandchildren of some really annoying people. Absolute wankers. They were parked on double yellow lines the other day, 'Only for five minutes' – TWO HOURS they were there, the tramps. Them too. You cut back consumption or organized a clean-up or wrote to a councillor or a company. You. You did all of that.

How many atmospheres had you repaired before? Actual atmospheres, not metaphorical ones where you realized *you* were the sound one at a particular weird wedding-dinner table? And you could be any kind of hero. An expert on policy, or defending campaigners from defamation suits, or good at working out how to organise thirty volunteers to put a path through a bog, or a Bruce Willis type in a grimy vest, all action and confidence confronting a mattress dumper, or a sharp-suited insider gradually eroding the Old Ways from the inside. You could have any number of skills or specialities and a vague feeling of wanting to do 'something'. What do you love, what are you good at, what needs to be done nearby?

Okay, maybe you're not arsed about life having much meaning, you might be nihilistic and say what's the point, we've lost so there's nothing to lose. Or you could be me, really good at worrying and inching painfully towards turning that worry to good use even with a side order of hypocrisy.

Either way, isn't it worth a shot?

11.

The Little book of Colm

I named a chapter after myself. The final act of ego. But it's short and might repeat a few things you've read already. Thinking about climate change and nature in trouble is not one long journey of enlightenment. It's frankly a pain in the hole. I wish I could think about something else. There are lots of times when I get very down and 'what's the point?'-y. The parade of bad news doesn't stop. The list of things I didn't know I had to worry about is added to daily. Most recently, it's fucking bird flu. Thousands of terns dying because they caught flu off our fucking chickens FOR FUCK SAKE. Terns, minding their own business just sitting in their colonies, serving food to their chicks, maybe alternating on the fish runs (waiting their tern, as it were) only to be killed by fucking flu got in some manky shed full of miserable barely sentient protein units that never see light or a butterfly, grown only for us to throw most of their bodies away unfinished in nugget form at a children's birthday party in FUNLAND SOFTPLAY. We deserve a fucking asteroid or a nuclear winter at this stage. But I won't be able to arrange that at short notice so to help in these glum times,

I arm myself with a list of imperfect inaccurate principles that might only work for me at the moment and need to be updated. Fifteen rules I'm living by for now, that mightn't work for you. But they might.

1. I'd rather be an eejit than a cynic

Some of this book is a bit pollyannish, a bit *"if we all get along we can really do it, people! Now, let's play some Christian guitar!"* Or as Captain Planet would say, *the power is YOURS*. Nagging away at the back of my brain is the distinct possibility that humanity is a gobshite that will not act in its own interests and we'll need both a revolution and apocalypse to make people look up from their phones. But for now, I reckon there's enough realists out there. The devil has enough advocates on his payroll, and enough people who think it's all virtue-signalling nonsense. So, I'm going to go with optimism for a while. If and when it's proven that there is no place for my type of wishy-washy broad engagement shite, I promise I will get my general diploma in Eating The Rich (or not getting eaten if things have gone well) .

2. You have to burn a bit of diesel to save a bit of diesel, but you should still keep track of it

A paper copy of this book costs about 2kg of CO_2. That's on me. I know the publishers have written something at the start about sustainable forests, but the most sustainable thing would be if this book didn't exist. Ebooks are bit better as long as you don't get a new device to read it. Audiobooks are the best. And you get to listen to my phone voice. But if every paper book sold is my fault, then this year I will roughly double my carbon footprint in the hope that it helps others lower theirs. This, it could be argued, is a loadabollox. But there are lots of environmental improvements that have a start-up cost. If this book is helpful in the 'conversation' then maybe in the long run it might have been worth it. And either way, I have a few tons of CO_2 to fix over the next while. Solar panels and planting about 300 trees is the target.

3. No disrespect intended, but I don't have the room for your bad news too

There are times where I just say, I can't listen to that bit of bad news now. There isn't room. I'm have fingers in my ears and I'm shouting LALALALALALA. I can't deal with that newt population collapse. I had just finished filing *"no one available to fight Siberian wildfires because of a pointless war"* in my brain. So, I'm sorry this other thing is happening, but it's not on my To-Worry list today.

4. I'm not competing with you, I'm competing with a different version of me

My 'journey' to help in all of this is not so I can feel smug compared to others. (Well, it is a bit, but not publicly. Discreet smugness is a hugely important mental vitamin for me.) But mainly I'm measuring progress against the Me who could easily do shag-all without anyone knowing.

5. Fatalism is handy for the dark times

When I get down about it all, I console myself that I tried, we're all going to die anyway, and ah lookit wasn't it a good run and the universe is really only destined for heat-death for 99.999999999% of its life and the 13 billion years from the Big Bang until the June 15th 2089 is but a blink of an eye. I don't spend long thinking this. It's purely a strategy to get me over a hump.

6. We have no time left to act and we have all the time in the world

A few years ago, the news was awash with the message that we have 12 years to save the planet. Yes, it got our attention, but I also felt like I wouldn't personally get much done and maybe it was already too late. So, to counteract that, I follow a better message which is that every single bit of a degree of warming that isn't 'baked into the atmosphere' is up for grabs and worth fighting for. Basically, I'm talking about avoiding relegation on goal difference even if we are playing shit. Keep scrapping.

7. Those who can, should, and they should do what they can

If you don't have the money, time, space, energy, health to do much at the moment don't feel bad. Those with any of the above should pick up the slack. Me included.

8. Please indicate before changing lane

There are bits here I don't know a whole lot about so I'm trying to teach myself to shut up until I do. Especially energy. How we are going to get the SQUIGGAWATTS needed to keep people warm and cook their food and generally transform entire economies. So, at the moment I'm not saying a whole lot about it. You probably know more than me. Read other books.

9. Don't be planting trees in the middle of someone's sunbathing patch

What I mean by this is, we all want to Do Something but we are not just Doing Something, we are representing an idea and we should be conscious of that too. So a wildflower patch is lovely and all but if the community associate it with neglect because they've been neglected before then we need to listen before thistling the place. Likewise if an area is mowed because children play in it and there's now a tree in the way, we're just making it look like Them Fucking

Environmentalists Are At It Again. Yes nature was there first but someone else was there second before we came along third. This is not a recipe for doing nothing. It's a recommendation for asking questions first.

10. Bolloxes have good ideas too

The hardest lesson I have yet to learn is that people I don't like can make good points too. This is really annoying. The big fucking head on them, being right. Bastards.

11. One day you'll need to build an extension too

This is a long game. I can be having rows with people now about dogshite in bags but I don't know when in my neighbourhood I might need their help on another matter. Sooner or later everyone needs their neighbour to give them a bit of slack when they have builders in kangoing the wall. So in this long game, we will disagree but that doesn't mean we won't need each other. Managing the balance between pragmatism and rows is something I'm still learning.

12. Ever tried. Ever failed. No matter. Try
    again. Fail again. Fail to prepare better,
    better fail to prepare, sitting up there with
    your prawn sandwiches . . .

Roy Keane and Samuel Beckett combining to sum up both
the rage at making a balls of this and still keeping going.
There will always be that extra car journey because fuckit
the *thought of getting on a bus now*, that filthy durty tasty
bit of processed meat when I'm feeling weak, that bag of
canal rubbish that wasn't collected and was then thrown
ironically back into the canal by The Youth of Today, that
time I chickened out of asking if someone wouldn't mind
not havin the engine running outside a school in the
middle of an oil crisis. As Anna says in Frozen 2, do the
next right thing.

13. Don't be tying yourself in knots making
    lists of rules for life with nice round
    numbers like fifteen. It puts too much
    pressure to just think of one to make up
    the numbers. The latter ones end up
    being rushed and without as much
    thought. The number of items on the list
    aren't important so you can end it any
    time

14. Actually no, wait. The little book of
    Colm list can change at any time. It's not
    definitive. Other things will be added to it
    from time to time so you should leave
    space for them

15. Space intentionally left blank for
    'personal growth'

Further Reading
(or, The Big Books of Not Colm)

I know nothing about nothing. My expertise is limited to ordering words in a particular way to try and make people laugh, and also picking up rubbish. For everything else I'm just learning on the job. But if it helps here are a few of the things I've been reading and listening to.

The Wizard and the Prophet by Charles C. Mann

If you find yourself thinking *well how are we going to feed everyone, well? WELL?* This book talks about how we got to the point of feeding 8 billion better than we used to feed 2 billion. It's about much more than that: solar panels, cold war intrigue, and two men who represented in the middle of the last century two ways of looking at agriculture in the world. One said we're eventually going to make this place a desert, the other said we will always invent our way out of it.

Feral by George Monbiot

Mention the name Monbiot to a lot of farmers and they will react as if you've just said that something has been worrying their sheep. It might even have been George himself worrying them. He reckons they are Mesopotamian invaders nibbling every last plant from the soil. Although he talks about Welsh mountains, reading this was when I started to look at Ireland's landscape differently. It's the first thing I read that made me wonder why our mountains have no trees. I don't know enough to say whether he or his detractors are right, but he writes bloody well, and after reading you will likely look around you in a different way.

Whittled Away by Padraig Fogarty

Get angry. We had loads of wildlife in this country. And fish. Where are all the fish gone? A stunning examination of what we had and what we have and what we could have in this country.

How to Talk About Climate Change by Rebecca Huntley

Another piece in the jigsaw puzzle of figuring out how to unmelt your head. In this book among other things, it looks at the problem in terms of the emotions we feel when we think and talk about climate change.

The Meat Paradox by Rob Percival

I was already thinking about the meat paradox before I read the book, but this is much more comprehensive than my few tuppence worth. He goes right up the nostrils of the question and what it means to eat meat. He pulls the trigger. He feels bad. Accompany him on every bit of this mental journey on what it means to eat another animal. I still eat meat after reading it, but this kind of thinking is good for the brain. A bit like meat is.

Less is More, How Degrowth Will Save the World by Jason Hickel

Let's not get caught up in the word *degrowth*. The basic premise of this book: that a planet which is finite cannot grow its economy forever would seem to make perfect sense, but some people get really angry about the concept. Often degrowthers are accused of wanting developing countries not to have their shot at development because we need to reduce everything now. That's not what they're saying, but it is a sort of heresy to challenge the idea that growing is automatically a good thing. Finite Planet, Infinite Growth. 2 into 0 won't go. Start with that and see how you get on.

The New Climate War by Michael E. Mann

This fella has been in the trenches. Documenting the misinformation and denial while also doing the actual science. What's interesting about this book is how climate denial has been replaced by more subtle tactics like climate deflection (which more closely resembles something I might do myself.) Know the signs.

How to Save a Planet – a podcast by Alex Goldberg and Dr Ayana Elizabeth Johnson

Podcasts are piling up. Most of them are shite. This is not shite. Nor is it gloom-laden. It is a good primer. I'm a big fan of the Doctor. She's a brilliant communicator and a proper scientist and she has assembled a great team of reporters. It's never not fascinating. Learn about seaweed and the mad world of people who will buy your old refrigerant off you.

All We Can Save edited by Ayana Elizabeth Johnson, Katherine K. Wilkinson

More from Dr Johnson. This time an anthology of writing about climate by women from all over the world. This book is great if you find that what you're reading has been written by The Same People Who Seem To Write All The Books, namely people who look like me. And the title is important. There is a lot to save. We need to focus on what we can save.

The Good Ancestor by Roman Krznaric

You could sum up the impact this book had on me in that for the first time in my life I thought of myself as a future ancestor in the real sense, not in the *will anyone visit my cold and lonely grave sense*. If you think we're all going to die anyway and what's the point, this book is a handy correction. It gently nudges you with the responsibility that you have, not just to the children you can see, but the future adults you can't.

The Uninhabitable Earth by David Wallace-Wells.

Hoo boy. Don't listen to this audio book in the gym. There is no point in continuing your planks unless you believe it'll help you in the After Times. But if you're able to stomach a necessary narration of how everything is fucked, and we need to do something about it very soon, this will set the mood.

Braiding Sweetgrass by Robin Kimmerer

Sometimes sad, sometimes funny, always gorgeous. An ecologist writes about her life and the nature she has lived with while she studied, and how her Potawatomi (Native American people from the Great Lakes) taught her to look differently at the world around her. The thing about this book is that an earlier version of me would have been too impatient, too cynical, too disinterested in nature to appreciate it. Enjoying this book is an example of how any oul bollox can grow into a richer understanding of something by giving it a bit of time.

The Physics of Climate Change by Lawrence M. Kraus

It's easy enough to understand a hard thing if someone takes you through the basics, and that's where I'm at after reading this book. I don't know how climate models work exactly but I do know most of them are producing roughly the same answers and I sort of understand why climate change might be happening, give or take, carry the four. As I mentioned earlier you would think I knew this stuff already, but I didn't. This book gives me a bit of confidence.

Any book about the End of the Universe.

If you're the type of person who is interested in when the universe ends and you realise that it will go on for the next 10 to the power of 100 to the power of something else-years and most of that time is just dark nothingness, the author will likely make the point: our entire universe to date is a blink of an eye, our planet is an absolute miracle of rarity. Wouldn't it be a shame if, against that massive backdrop, we just made shite of the place?

The books I didn't read (yet).

I haven't read enough fiction, writing by farmers, by manufacturers, by energy experts, people from places most affected by climate collapse, or in general books by people I'm likely to disagree with. But I'm not finished.

Acknowledgements

Thanks to my wife, Marie, and my children, Ruby and Lily, who are patient when I go around pointlessly switching off lights and supportive when I'm rage-picking rubbish and generally lovely people to spend my life with.

To my editor, Catherine, who right from the first meeting 'got it', even though I wasn't entirely clear about what 'it' was. To Kerri and Stephen, who took over as editors when Catherine embarked on a lifelong project of her own, and guided me to the end.

To Faith and the team at the Lisa Richards agency who, especially during a tricky two years for 'crowds-funded' people like me, were a huge support as I hustled and Zoomed and odd-jobbed until the venues opened again.

And finally to all the people who give a shit and do a bit (especially in Inchicore and Dripsey :)), , whatever your job or background, in or out of high-vis, thanked or not thanked, paid or unpaid, whether your thing is rubbish or water or air or data or animals or trees or unloved little weeds or crows or freedom of information requests or health or driving public transport, thanks for all you do. Lots of us see and hear you.